Cactus and Succulents

By the Editors of Sunset Books and Sunset Magazine

Lane Publishing Co., Menlo Park, California

The fleshy and the ferocious...

It is difficult, if not impossible, to think of any group of plants that compares in versatility to cacti and succulents. What other plant group claims so many intriguing shapes and spectacular blooms, yet still has such a carefree, rugged, unthirsty nature? From striking ornamentals and ferociously spined barrels to clustering rosettes, ground covers, and climbing vines, succulents—cacti and certain "fleshy" families that store water within themselves—can easily fit into almost any garden environment. And many cacti have the added plus of being able to adapt readily to indoor planting situations.

For their valuable assistance in the research for this book, a special thanks to Jim Daniel, C. W. Kreiss, and George and Carol Scannell. Our appreciation, also, to the following nurseries: Tanque Verde Greenhouses (Tucson), Desert Nursery (Riverside, California), Roger's Gardens (Newport Beach, California), and Cactus Gem Nursery (Cupertino, California).

Edited by Linda Brandt

Design: Alan May

Illustrations: Marcia Kier-Hawthorne

Cover: Field-grown specimens of *Echinocactus grusonii* (foreground) and *Agave parrasana*. Photographed by Steve W. Marley.

Editor, Sunset Books: David E. Clark

Fourth printing June 1982

Contents

Special features

CACTUS and other SUCCULENTS

An example of nature's ingenuity in adapting to environmental extremes.

Flattened pads of opuntia

Fleshy rosette of echeveria

Columnar growth of cleistocactus

"Survival of the fittest" is no more accurately shown than by the changes within the succulent world. As the earth evolved, rivers and oceans receded, causing most plant life to weaken and finally succumb. But there were a few survivors. By some chance, they managed to exist in the drying wastelands, adapting and protecting themselves in remarkably ingenious ways.

Some succulents developed a more compact body, shortening leaves and stems to almost nothing. They became spherical or low growing, reducing their surface area and thus the rate of moisture evaporation. Others, eager to arm themselves against herbivorous predators, adapted differently. Look at a commonly grown succulent. How do you think it managed to adapt? Can you guess which physical characteristics might have helped that plant survive?

The cactus, agave, and aloe grew sharp bristles and hooked, ferocious spines. Gasterias and other fleshy succulents developed thick skins too tough for hungry animals to penetrate. Some inventive species produced foul-tasting, often poisonous juices. Others simply moved away from the area altogether; they either became epiphytes (tree dwellers), clinging to moss or the bark of trees, or cleverly hid in the deep crevices of large, protective rocks.

One last group—unanimously chosen the most ingenious—disguised themselves by mimicking their surroundings. Instead of looking like plants, they resemble polished pebbles and old weathered rocks. Only their names—flowering stones and living rocks—hint of their secret, double life.

A succulent is just a...

Almost all plants manufacture food. A few also have the ability to store nourishing ingredients. Succulents (from the Latin word *succos,* meaning juice) store the most essential ingredient needed for survival—water. Within

Angled stems of epiphyllum | Overlapping leaves of sedum | Spectacular bloom of echinopsis

their swollen leaves, stems, and roots, succulent plants house all the moisture needed for long periods of drought. It is this unique ability that enables them to survive the most hostile environments.

Where did they come from?

Which are the native habitats of succulents—desert wastelands, mountain tops, jungles, or near oceans?

You may be surprised to learn that all of these answers are correct. The deserts of the world contain most—but by no means all—of the succulents.

Many succulents developed in the cold alpine regions of Europe where they adjusted to strong winds and poor, rocky soil. From the tropical jungles of Central and South America came another kind of succulent—epiphytes. Rainfall in this area was high and so were the plants. Tree-dwelling species collected nourishment and moisture from surrounding moss and bark.

A final group of succulents, living on the shores of salt water lakes and oceans, developed because the salt water concentration was so high that pure water was difficult to find. There is practically no area in the world where some form of succulent didn't survive.

Likewise, almost any environment is suitable for growing some kind of succulent plant. You may live in the desert where temperatures remain warm and dry, in tropical or rainy areas that are consistently damp and humid, or in the mountains or parts of the country where temperatures drop below freezing with predictable regularity. Any of these locations·are conducive to raising cacti and succulents—success merely depends on choosing the right ones.

Take a look at the assortment

The cactus family is just one of many groups called succulent plants. As you read further, you'll discover that daisies, lilies, geraniums, and even grapes have species that are considered succulent plants. But for now, let's take a look at the assortment the larger families have to offer.

Cacti, euphorbias, crassulas, milkweeds, lilies, agaves, and more—all are succulents and all managed to survive, but each appears distinctively different. Look at the illustrations on pages 4 and 5; they are examples of just a few different kinds of succulent plants.

Whether you enjoy them for their flowers, foliage, or form, cacti and succulents are a new world of plants for you to discover. We think they are the most fascinating group in the entire plant kingdom.

How plants get their names

Carl von Linne, also known as Linnaeus, devised a system of categorizing plants and animals into specific groups. Large groups are known as **genera** (genus is the singular form); more specific smaller ones are called **species.** Together these botanical breakdowns help us to identify plants according to families—all of which share certain characteristics.

To some people, calling plants by their botanical name seems unnecessary. It's true—Latin names are confusing and can be difficult to pronounce. However, unlike common names that may mean one thing to a cactus grower in Phoenix and something completely different to a collector in Minneapolis, botanical names are reliably accurate.

One of the most fascinating things about plant nomenclature is the reasoning behind it: plants are usually given names for a specific reason. It may be to describe their appearance, their growth habit, where they were first discovered, or who discovered them.

Look at the name of the popular cactus, *Cephalocereus senilis* (*sef-ah-loh-see-ree-us sen-ill-us*). If we told you that **cephalo** refers to the head, **cereus** suggests a tall, candle-like appearance, and **senilis** means old or white-haired, could you visualize what this cactus should look like? Turn to pages 15 and 16 and see how you did. *Cephalocereus senilis,* more commonly called old man cactus, is indeed a tall, candle-shaped cactus covered with a mass of white woolly hair.

When you come across a cactus with a name like *Trichocereus peruvianus,* you would be correct in assuming that its native habitat is Peru. And, that *Euphorbia horrida* (see page 39) is, in fact, somewhat ferocious. Likewise, *Echinocactus horizonthalonius,* better known as Mexican mule crippler because of its spreading, horizontal growth habit, is used as a barrier to keep animals from straying too far.

But what about names like *Agave victoriae-reginae* and *Selenicereus macdonaldiae?* Perhaps Selenicereus sounds like Latin—but macdonaldiae?

We mentioned that plants can be named for people. It's quite common, in fact, for a new species to have the same name as its discoverer. For example, if Olivia Johnson discovered a rare species of *Opuntia* near Omaha and wanted to name it after herself, she might call it *Opuntia oliviae* (in Latin, *-ae* is the feminine ending). On the other hand, if she wanted to include her husband in on the festivities, she could call her discovery *Opuntia johnsonii* (*-ii* ending is the masculine form).

However, if by some chance another cactus collector found a rare species of *Opuntia* and christened it with the identical name—only one week earlier—Olivia would have to try again. The rules say that no two plants can be given the same botanical name. But Olivia need not give up so easily; she could always call it *Opuntia omahensis.* After all, she did find it near Omaha.

We will be mentioning words like **family, genus, species,** and **variety** throughout the book. These terms will be clearer if you understand how the names relate:

One variety or more make up a species

One species or more make up a genus

One genus or more make up a family

In a name like *Opuntia microdasys rufida,* Opuntia is the genus, *microdasys* is the species, and *rufida* is the variety. The family, of course, is the cactus.

Stuck on an unfamiliar word?

Cactus terminology can be a real stickler. To many readers, words like "glochid," "tubercle," and "areole"

---

native species

...it's vital to protect them

During the last decade and particularly within the last few years, we've witnessed an increasing demand for succulent plants. Unfortunately, such demands can leave scars on the landscape and often enough, rare and endangered species of cacti are the victims.

Although some of the largest threats to endangered species come from commercial exploitation, new housing construction—even from agriculture and grazing animals—we, as individuals, can help by curbing our own field collecting.

If you do collect cactus, here are a few thoughts to keep in mind:

1. Before collecting any plants, investigate local laws. In some areas, knowingly removing endangered or threatened species can result in a substantial fine.

2. Check to see if a permit is necessary. Many permits specifically state just which plants can be collected.

3. Do as little damage to surrounding areas as possible.

4. Whenever possible, collect seeds or offsets rather than the entire plant. Remember that mature specimens rarely transplant well and are needed much more to produce seed for regeneration.

various parts of a cactus

(no specific one)

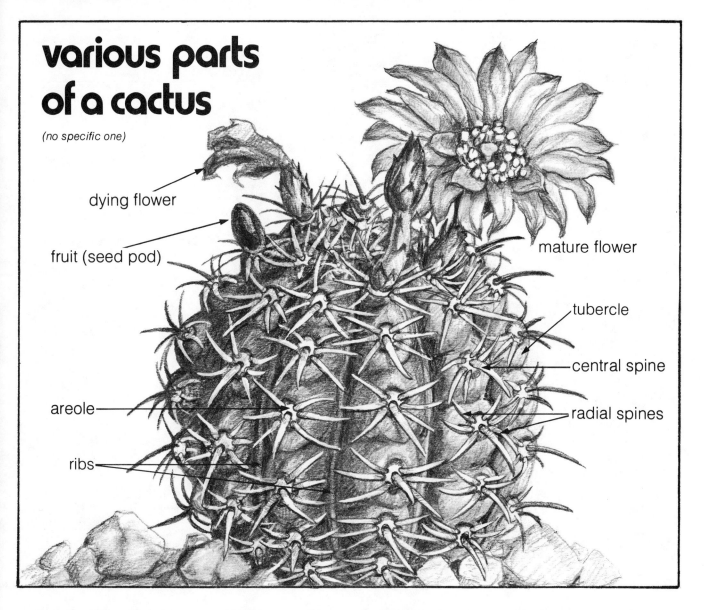

dying flower

fruit (seed pod)

areole

ribs

mature flower

tubercle

central spine

radial spines

mean very little. Since most cactus books (including ours) refer to these anatomical parts of plants often, we've listed some descriptive terms to help you. Along with the diagram above, our informative mini-encyclopedia is guaranteed to sharpen your understanding of cactus terminology.

Appressed: Flattened or closely pressed against.

Areole: The area on a cactus stem or branch where spines and flowers are produced.

Cephalium: Mass of bristles and wool that develops at top of a cactus. Found on melocactus and discocactus species.

Epidermis: The outer skin or top layer of cells on a plant.

Epiphytes: Tree-dwelling plants that live in branch crotches, gathering moisture and nutrients from surrounding moss and bark.

Free-flowering: Profuse bloomer. A cactus that blooms easily (without special care) and prolifically.

Fruit: The ovary (seed-bearing part) of the flower that swells and ripens, housing seeds inside.

Glochid: Small tufts of barbed hair or stickers. Mostly found on opuntias.

Hair: See Wool.

Hybridize: To crossbreed one kind of plant with another.

Propagate: A method of reproduction, resulting in more plants. Methods include planting seeds, taking cuttings, dividing plants at roots or offsets, and grafting.

Rib: Ridges that form the outer edges of a cactus.

Spine: Bristles, stickers, or thorns. Radial spines surround one or more central spines.

Tubercle: Nipplelike projection (called a "chin" on some species) whose tip bears the areole.

Wool: Hair, growing from plant. On some species of *Cephalocereus,* hair is long and flowing; on others, it's short and thick.

The Cactus Collection

You can easily identify cactus. With rare exceptions (such as the primitive *Pereskia* and its close relatives), most do not have leaves, or when any are present, they soon fall off. Though most of them have spines and bristles, there are even some cacti without spines; several have long hair or a woolly covering instead.

Identifying a cactus

We mentioned that all cacti are succulents, but all spiny succulent plants are *not* cacti. This may sound confusing, but there's an easy way to tell the difference.

First, examine the plant, asking two questions: does it have any spines or sharply pointed hairs? If so, are they arranged in clusters separated by areas of spineless skin? If the answers to both questions are yes, the plant most likely is a cactus. If one or both characteristics are missing, you may have a succulent plant but certainly not a cactus.

If you're still a bit confused, look at the pattern or arrangement of spines. Botanically, only cacti have *areoles*—small pores or discs where spines and flowers originate. Often these spine clusters are arranged in rows along raised ridges, as in barrel cacti and saguaro. In most cases, though, the areoles are randomly scattered, organized only by the fairly uniform spacing between them. Each areole usually bears multiple spines. In other spiny succulents, the spines or thorns are solitary—rarely occurring in clusters.

One last feature about cacti may help you in identification: flowers originate from the areoles. Usually funnel-shaped with a flaring mouth, most blooms have a large but indefinite number of stamens—often more than 50.

Three different tribes

Three tribes of cacti are named by modern taxonomists: *Pereskieae, Opuntieae,* and *Cereeae.* Though all are members of the cactus family, the pereskias are often singled out because of their distinct appearance and rigid growing requirements.

We mention the pereskias briefly here; the remainder of the cactus chapter is devoted to the more varied, attractive, and hardy plants within the Opuntia and Cereus families. Both of these families are broken down further into genera with growing requirements, average height at maturity, blooming season, and safe, minimum winter temperatures given for each.

Primitive pereskias

The primitive, leafy pereskias appear to be the last link between cacti, as we recognize them today, and other evergreen plants. Like other cacti, they have both areoles and spines—straight ones for protection and hooked ones for climbing. But that's where the similarities stop.

They grow as common jungle vines and shrubby trees, and because of their thorny, woody stems and sprawling habit, resemble rose bushes more than cacti. In tropical areas of South and Central America and parts of Mexico where conditions are ideal, pereskias reach a height of 10 feet or more and are covered with hundreds of colorful, trumpet-shaped flowers in autumn. Unfortunately, in cultivation, they usually remain small and fail to bloom at all.

Some species—usually the ones with thick, juicy leaves—are evergreen; thin-leafed varieties are often deciduous and, therefore, fairly unattractive during the dormant period. In their native habitat, pereskias are trained into hedging plants, but elsewhere they should be considered only tender greenhouse specimens.

There are more than 15 different pereskia species; the most common are:

Pereskia aculeata (LEMON VINE). Sometimes raised for its fruit, called Barbados gooseberries, this pereskia is most widely cultivated. It has a sprawling, vining habit, reaching 12 feet tall; tiny, strongly scented flowers are white, yellow, sometimes pink. Slender stems bear needle-shaped spines on mature plants.

P. bleo (WAX ROSE). Tree-size habit, reaching 15 feet or more. Rose-colored flowers. May be used as understock for grafting epiphyllums.

Opuntia basilaris (beaver tail cactus)

Opuntia 'Santa Rita'

Yellow-flowering opuntia

Flower of *Opuntia acanthocarpa*

Opuntia...

jointed pads, barbed bristles, haphazard growth

Opuntia bigelovii (teddy bear cactus)

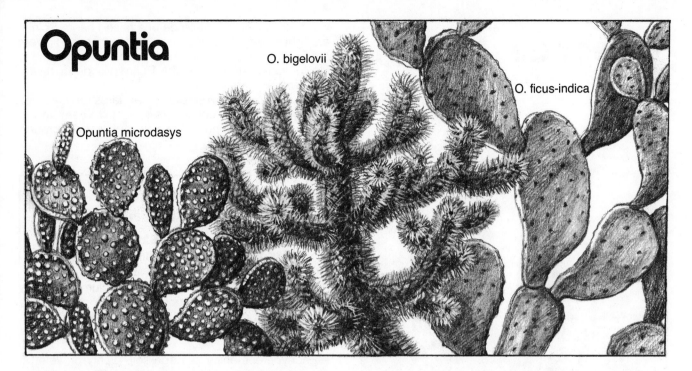

Opuntia

O. bigelovii

O. ficus-indica

Opuntia microdasys

When you examine the genus *Opuntia*, you'll notice three distinct groups based on growth form: the prickly pears that have flat-jointed pads, one growing out of the other; the tall cylindrical-jointed chollas; and the dwarf species with globular or cylindrical stems.

Opuntia	
Chollas, Prickly Pears	
Height: 2–15′	**Blooms:** Spring, summer
Exposure: Sun	**Hardiness:** 35°F.

Planted singly or in groups in spacious natural settings, many opuntias make exciting landscape subjects. Most species grow rapidly and are free-flowering with blooms of yellow, white, orange, purple, or red. They do need room to grow freely because sharp bristles and spines can be quite hazardous in small gardens. (See page 75 for a painless way to remove bristles from your finger.)

Indoors, potted opuntias like *O. microdasys* are perfect as house plants in a sunny window garden—just make sure they get sufficient light to prevent branches from becoming spindly and misshapen. Don't be too discouraged if your plant fails to bloom; potted opuntias rarely get large enough to produce many flowers.

We describe these popular and useful opuntias:

Opuntia acanthocarpa (BUCKHORN CHOLLA). Rare species. Springtime reddish blooms. (Photo on facing page.)

O. basilaris (BEAVER TAIL). Flat, nearly spineless, gray or purplish pads characterize this opuntia. Low branching to 4 feet. Can be found throughout much of the United States and northern Mexico. Blooms range from most common purple to carmine, pink, sometimes yellow. (Photo on facing page.)

O. bigelovii (TEDDY BEAR CACTUS). A native to Arizona, Nevada, and California, this treelike cactus has a woolly trunk covered with vicious silvery yellow spines. Flowers, appearing in early spring, are pale green, yellow, or white marked with lavender. An attractive desert plant that grows freely yet slowly (2–8 feet) in hottest, driest deserts. (Photo on facing page.)

O. ficus-indica (INDIAN FIG). Often grown for its fruit, this shrubby cactus has a woody trunk and smooth, gray, flat joints. Yellow flowers appear in spring or early summer. Edible, good-size fruits are either yellow or red. Handle carefully—bristles break off easily.

O. microdasys (BUNNY EARS). A popular house plant, this beautiful Mexican dwarf species has flat, oblong, spineless pads covered with tufts of golden bristles called glochids. Available in many varieties, all with variously colored glochids ranging from white on *O. m.* 'Albispina' (POLKA DOT) to reddish brown on *O. m. rufida*.

O. prolifera (JUMPING CHOLLA). Erect cactus, 3–8 feet tall, has reddish brown spines and easily detached joints. Rose to purple flowers appear in spring or summer.

O. ramosissima (PENCIL CHOLLA, DARNING NEEDLE CHOLLA). Extremely rare. Inconspicuous flowers hide deep within spines, open for a matter of hours during hottest part of day.

O. vulgaris. Large, treelike, tropical or subtropical cactus. Variety *O. v.* 'Variegata' is popularly nicknamed Joseph's coat cactus because of its strange markings—some joints are green, some white or yellow, others mottled.

Cereanae

Carnegiea
gigantea

Stetsonia
coryne

Pachycereus
pringlei

The tribe *Cereeae* can be broken into subtribes. Within the subtribe *Cereanae* are: *Carnegiea, Pachycereus, Stetsonia, Cereus, Lemaireocereus, Lophocereus, Trichocereus, Cephalocereus, Espostoa, Cleistocactus, Heliocereus.*

Carnegiea
A Candelabra Cactus

Height: To 60' | **Blooms:** Spring, summer
Exposure: Sun | **Hardiness:** 25°F.

The genus *Carnegiea* has only one species.

Carnegiea gigantea (SAGUARO). Found in southwest Arizona and parts of Sonora, Mexico, saguaros are among the largest, slowest-growing cacti known. Mature specimens may take a century or more to reach their treelike stature. (Photo on page 15.)

Columnar, fluted ribs on stout branches curve up-

ward, giving the appearance of a raised hand. Spines are light brown. Greenish white, night-blooming flowers are fragrant and appear on mature plants sometime in May or early June. Oval, edible fruits split open to reveal red pulp.

Because they grow so slowly, saguaros remain small enough to grow in containers for many years. In the landscape, mature cacti make a dramatic background for outdoor plantings.

Pachycereus
A Candelabra Cactus

Height: To 70' | **Blooms:** Spring
Exposure: Sun | **Hardiness:** 35°F.

A Mexican native, this easy-to-grow columnar cactus has a number of treelike species. Confined to a greenhouse or indoors, young plants make attractive potted subjects. Outdoors, plants grow tall, then branch outward.

Pachycereus enjoy average soil, plenty of water in hot weather, and protection from frost. If temperatures drop too close to freezing during a wet winter, plants can become misshapen or distorted. Like other night-blooming cereus, flowers first open about 10 p.m. and remain open all night; they close about 11 a.m. If weather is overcast, some remain open for 2 full days.

Pachycereus pecten-aboriginum (INDIAN COMB, HAIRBRUSH CACTUS). Often a giant—up to 35 feet or more. Stiff branches are thick, erect. White flowers appear only on mature plants. The fruit—about the size of a baseball—is covered with long, stiff golden spines and was used by local Indians as a comb.

P. pringlei (MEXICAN GIANT, ELEPHANT CACTUS). Columnar growth to 70 feet characterizes this best-known species. Cactus has woody trunk, ribbed branches, white springtime flowers. The world's largest cactus.

Stetsonia
A Candelabra Cactus

Height: To 25' | **Blooms:** Spring
Exposure: Sun | **Hardiness:** 35°F.

The genus *Stetsonia* has only one species.

Stetsonia coryne (TOOTHPICK CACTUS). An excellent potted plant suitable for greenhouse or indoors when young, but like many cereus species, eventually grows to treelike size. Beautiful spination—each areole contains black central spine surrounded by long white radial spines. Funnel-shaped white flowers are nocturnal and can be expected only on mature cacti.

Toothpick cactus requires an average soil mixture and watering. Plant is fairly tender and should be kept well protected from frost during winter.

Lemaireocereus
thurberi

Trichocereus spachianus

More Cereus

Cereus peruvianus
'Monstrosus'

Cereus
A Candelabra Cactus

Height: To 30'   **Blooms:** Summer
Exposure: Sun   **Hardiness:** 30°F.

Cereanae comes from the Greek word for "wax candle;" the name seems most appropriate when you look at this tall, columnar cactus. Its nocturnal white flowers illuminate the top as if in flames.

All of the cereus species are easy to grow, and because they are strong, vigorous plants, they have become a natural choice for grafting stock. When young, they grow into straight columns but often miniature if left in pots over the years. Outdoors in the landscape, they become tree-size cacti, often reaching 30 feet or more. Some form a candelabra-shaped crown; others branch at the base. Because most cereus can easily be raised from seed, much hybridizing has occurred. (See photo at lower left, page 15.)

Cereus hildmannianus. A native of Brazil, this tall, columnar, treelike cactus may reach 20 feet. Large white flowers, 8–9 inches long.

C. jamacaru. Needle-shaped yellowish spines (often 10–15 growing from each areole) and bluish green stems characterize this cereus. Nocturnal white flowers.

C. peruvianus (PERUVIAN APPLE, PERUVIAN TORCH). Most common of all cereus, this cactus can be either shrubby (to 10 feet) or reach tree size. Its branches are bluish green with brown or black needle-shaped spines. Nocturnal 7-inch white flowers appear in June and are lightly fragrant.

C. p. 'Longispinus' (APPLE CACTUS). Beautiful, nocturnal flowers are white around pale yellow stamens; rose pink tinges the outer guard petals. At maturity,

apple cactus has a stout central 6-inch shaft with such deeply indented ribs that it appears square. In summer, flower buds appear on plants that are at least 10 years old. Though each bloom lasts only one night, new flowers continue to open from July through September. Cuttings root well if thoroughly dried and set in a box of sand.

C. p. 'Monstrosus' (CURIOSITY PLANT). Smaller, slower growing with about a dozen ribs, irregularly broken and shaped like crests or knobs. Quite a conversation piece when potted and displayed indoors.

Lemaireocereus
An Organ Pipe Cactus

Height: To 25'   **Blooms:** Spring
Exposure: Sun   **Hardiness:** 35°F.

Lemaireocereus belongs to a group of cacti called organ pipe. They are tall, columnar plants that branch just above ground into many ribbed stems. The tropical species are more difficult to grow outdoors because they require high winter temperatures. The North American natives listed below are fairly hardy, requiring a sunny location and minimum winter temperatures above 35°F.

Lemaireocereus gummosus (DAGGER CACTUS). Shrubby growth to 15 feet with either erect or sprawling branches. Gray radial and central spines. Both 6-inch flowers and flesh of edible fruit are purple. (Also sold as *Machaerocereus gummosus*).

L. marginatus (ORGAN PIPE CACTUS). This fast-growing cactus, reaching 20 feet or more, branches at base just above ground. Dark green, erect stems are white-margined and prominently ribbed with small, stiff spines. Flowers, sometimes paired, are tubular and grow from tops of stems. Often used in hedges as barrier plant.

L. thurberi (ORGAN PIPE CACTUS). A native of Arizona and parts of Mexico, this lemaireocereus shares the common name organpipe cactus with *L. marginatus.* Ribbed, columnar cactus, sometimes branching from base, eventually reaches 15–20 feet. Dark, gray green stems, usually with 12–17 ribs, produce short, black spines. White-edged, purplish flowers bloom at night throughout May and June; then followed by edible red fruit. Attractive seedlings make suitable potted plants for indoors or out. (Photo on facing page.)

Lophocereus
An Organ Pipe Cactus

Height: To 15′   **Blooms:** Spring, summer

Exposure: Sun   **Hardiness:** 25°F.

This attractive native of southern Arizona and Sonora, Mexico, requires practically no care. Stout, columnar stems branch at base to form short trunk. Lophocereus have a unique appearance—each areole on flowering (or fertile) parts of cactus bears dozens of bristlelike spines and two or more small, nocturnal flowers. Flower colors range from white through pink, sometimes red.

Lophocereus schottii (WHISKER CACTUS). Erect stems, branching just above ground, may reach 15 feet tall, 8 inches thick. Radial, gray spines are conical, slightly larger at base, and surround a single, central spine. Upper areoles have twisted, bristlelike spines 1–4 inches long and produce small pink flowers in spring, summer.

L. s. 'Monstrosus' (TOTEM POLE CACTUS). Nearly spineless ribs are irregularly spaced, are almost knobby in appearance, and present a most unusual sight.

Trichocereus
An Organ Pipe Cactus

Height: To 20′   **Blooms:** Spring, summer

Exposure: Sun   **Hardiness:** 25°F.

Easy-to-grow cylindrical cacti, known for their hardiness, can grow to tree size, though many species remain small, indoor subjects if potted early in seedling stage. Their tidy appearance makes them suitable for well-lighted window gardens, lath houses, or greenhouses. Most have funnel-shaped, nocturnal white flowers; some mature species bloom in cultivation if raised outdoors in the garden. Because trichocereus are native to the Andes, often growing at high alpine altitudes, their hardiness has made them particularly popular as the understock for grafted cactus.

Trichocereus fascicularis (known as *Weberbauerocereus fascicularis*). Close-set areoles and needlelike yellow or brown short spines characterize this cactus. (A unique example of this genus is *Weberbauerocereus winterianus* shown on page 50.)

T. peruvianus (PERUVIAN TORCH). This Peruvian native has thick, multibranched stems that reach to 15 feet. Large areoles set an inch apart bear short, brown spines. Large flowers are white, nocturnal. Suitable as house plant if grown in well-lighted area.

T. spachianus (GOLDEN TORCH). Strong columnar growth to 7 feet, dividing at base to produce branches parallel to main stem. Needle-shaped spines are yellow to brown—8–10 radial spines surround single, thick central one. Because these spines are short, this species is most often used as an understock for grafting other cacti. Like other trichocereus, flowers are large and white.

Cephalocereus
An Old Man Cactus

Height: To 40′   **Blooms:** Spring
Exposure: Sun, partial shade   **Hardiness:** 40°F.

This is one of the most popular cacti for beginning collectors. The familiar old man cactus exemplifies this group: tall columnar or branching growth, usually covered by long, white woolly hair. Mature plants—some reach 40 feet in ideal surroundings—bear many nocturnal flowers on upper extremities. Rarely will indoor specimens flower, so most species are raised for their interesting appearance rather than profusion of blooms.

Cephalocereus prefer a typical cactus soil mixture (see page 75) and average watering during warm weather. Groom woolly hairs on your cephalocereus as you would your own: when hair becomes matted, carefully "shampoo" it in weak, soapy (not detergent) solution and rinse thoroughly, combing out any excess soap. Most species easily propagate from cuttings or seeds when started in a mixture of half sand and half soil. (For more propagating techniques, see page 74.)

Cephalocereus chrysacanthus (GOLDEN SPINES). Shrubby plant of ribbed, bluish stems grows to 15 feet. Bright yellow spines exposed through thick hairy wool. Flowers are rose colored and 3 inches long.

C. fulviceps (MEXICAN GIANT). A native to southern Mexico, this multibranched giant species can reach 50 feet tall, up to 1 foot thick. Bluish stems covered with brown woolly hair; flowers are white.

C. palmeri (WOOLLY TORCH, BILLY GOAT, BALD OLD MAN). Hardy plant with short, blue green spines and tufts of long, white, woolly hair. Columnar growth, then branching, up to 20 feet or more. Three-inch-long flowers are purplish brown.

Flower of *Lemaireocereus thurberi*

Cereus...

tall torches or branched, candelabra shapes

Lemaireocereus thurberi (organ pipe cactus)

Carnegiea gigantea (saguaro)

Flower of *Wilcoxia schmollii*

Cephalocereus senilis (old man cactus)

More Cereus

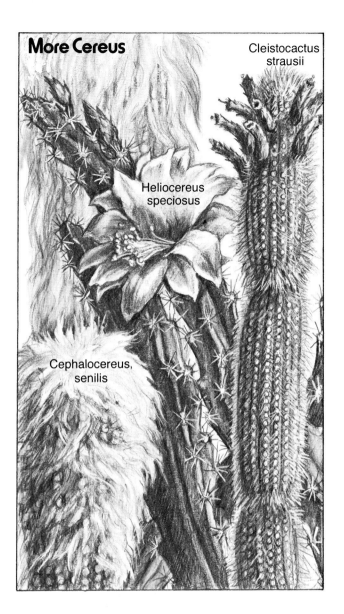

Cleistocactus strausii

Heliocereus speciosus

Cephalocereus, senilis

C. senilis (OLD MAN CACTUS). Slender, columnar cactus, may branch at base; slow growing to an eventual 40 feet, though usually much less. Tufts of long, grayish white hairs often hide 1½-inch yellow spines. Older plants produce nocturnal rose-colored flowers, usually in April or May. A fascinating potted plant for indoors or greenhouses; older plants are striking in cactus garden. Protect from hard frosts. (Photo on page 15.)

Espostoa
An Old Man Cactus

Height: To 15′ **Blooms:** Rarely
Exposure: Sun **Hardiness:** 45°F.

Known by many common names, this genus is a close relative to *Cephalocereus*. Characterized by its multiribbed, cylindrical growth, it differs most in the appearance of its flowers: they are funnel-shaped, covered even on stamens with scales and auxiliary hairs.

Espostoa lanata (COTTON BALL, PERUVIAN SNOW-BALL, PERUVIAN OLD MAN). Attractive, yellow-spined cactus is completely covered with fluffy, white, almost silky hair. Wool appears to grow in spiral manner. A fine potted plant for indoors, lath houses, or greenhouses. Usually grown for its interesting appearance rather than profusion of blooms; flowers appear only on mature plants and are often hidden by hair.

E. melanostele. Large, thick cylindrical cactus bears areoles with brown wool. Numerous, inch-long, black, radial spines surround single, stouter central one.

E. ulei. Treelike species may reach 15 feet tall or more. Unusual cephalium on top.

Cleistocactus
A Slender Torch Cactus

Height: To 10′ **Blooms:** Spring, summer
Exposure: Sun **Hardiness:** 35°F.

Some species of this slender, ribbed cactus grow to 10 feet; all are recognizable by a definite narrowing of the stem near growing point. Stems are usually no more than 3 inches thick, often leaning, and so thickly covered with spines that the stem surface is hardly visible. Tubular, orange red flowers are profuse, even in greenhouses, making *Cleistocactus* an attractive, easy-to-grow genus.

Cleistocactus baumannii (SCARLET BUGLER). Stiff, erect stems reach 6 feet, topped with yellowish spines. Bright orange to scarlet flowers are S-shaped and have a long blooming period.

C. jujuyensis. Attractive scarlet, tubular flowers appear in spring, summer. Colorful spination—brown to yellow—contrasts with light woolly hair.

C. strausii (SILVER TORCH). Upright plant of clustering columns that branch just above ground. This attractive, fast-growing variety produces dark red 4-inch flowers, usually in late spring.

Heliocereus
A Slender Torch Cactus

Height: To 5′ **Blooms:** Spring
Exposure: Partial shade **Hardiness:** 40°F.

Stems of this unusual tropical genus are bushy and erect; branches are strongly ribbed and four-angled. Because heliocereus are native to the tropics, they require a rich soil, ample moisture, and warmer temperatures than most cacti. In winter, locate in a bright spot that is kept completely protected.

Heliocereus speciosus (SUN CACTUS). Showy scarlet flowers up to 6 inches wide bloom in spring.

Echinocereanae

Echinocereus pectinatus

E. reichenbachii

Chamaecereus sylvestri

Nicknamed hedgehog cacti, *Echinocereanae* is another subtribe of the *Cereeae* tribe. We include *Echinocereus, Chamaecereus, Lobivia, Echinopsis,* and *Rebutia.*

Echinocereus
A Hedgehog Cactus

Height: To 15"

Exposure: Sun, partial shade

Blooms: Spring, summer

Hardiness: 25°F.

Echinocereus can be described as free-branching clusters or mounds of erect stems, sometimes prostrate, and usually less than a foot tall. All have highly ornamental spines which densely cover the plant surfaces. Large, showy flowers, to 4 inches across, are long lasting and appear on stems at the base or from the sides of the plant. As potted plants, echinocereus are enormously popular—their easy culture and overall tidy, compact appearance make them a welcome addition to any collection.

Echinocereus baileyi. See *E.r. albispinus.*

Echinocereus ehrenbergii. Stems erect, free-branching from base with slender, glassy white or light yellow spines; purple flowers.

E. engelmanii. Striking, hot pink or magenta flowers contrast with soft yellow spines. (Photo on page 18.)

E. enneacanthus (STRAWBERRY CACTUS). Thick stems grow in clumps, reach 1 foot tall. Needle-shaped, radial spines are transparent white; central spines, brown or gray. Reddish purple flowers appear in spring.

E. papillosus. Most unusual species. Flowers have fluorescent appearance; yellow or off-white petals tinged with red. (Photo on page 18.)

E. pectinatus. Thick, single stems, sometimes branched from the base, are covered with flattened, white radial spines. Summer flowers are magenta to yellow.

E. p. neomexicanus (RAINBOW CACTUS). Small, columnar plant densely covered with soft spines; large yellow blooms.

E. p. rigidissimus (RAINBOW CACTUS). This variety produces spines which form variously colored horizontal bands around the stems. Magenta flowers, up to 4 inches across, appear in spring.

E. reichenbachii (LACE CACTUS). Small, clumping cactus so heavily spined that it appears to have a lacy covering. Flowers are pink to purple, 3 inches wide, and appear in spring.

E. r. albispinus. Long, colorful radial spines; areoles narrowly elliptic.

Chamaecereus
Peanut Cactus

Height: To 1'

Exposure: Sun, partial shade

Blooms: Spring, summer

Hardiness: 25°F.

Showy, bright scarlet flowers will appear even indoors on this small, low-growing cactus. Its dwarfed appearance is characteristically cylindrical, ribbed, and spiny. Short joints branch from the base to produce a clumping, fingerlike effect. Its unusual shape and abundance

Echinopsis hybrids

Lobivia hybrid

Echinocereus engelmanii

Echinocereus...

delicate spination and
spectacular blooms

Pink-flowering rebutia hybrid

Echinocereus papillosus

Chamaecereus sylvestrii hybrid

of flowers—first appearing when cactus is quite young—make chamaecereus one of the most popular of all cacti.

Because joints fall off easily and root, propagating this cactus is rather simple. Much hybridizing has occurred; they are often crossed with different lobivias because they produce a variety of free-flowering novelties. (An unusual hybrid of *Chamaecereus* appears on the facing page.)

There is only one true species of *Chamaecereus*:

Chamaecereus sylvestrii (PEANUT CACTUS). Dense clusters of short, pale green branches are covered with small, white spines. Funnel-shaped blooms are bright red, up to 3 inches long, and appear on stout stems.

Lobivia
A Hedgehog Cactus

Height: To 1′   **Blooms:** Spring
Exposure: Sun,   **Hardiness:** 25°F.
partial shade

Nicknamed cob cactus, these small globular or cylindrical cacti have large showy flowers that often appear to be as big as the plants. Flower colors range from shades of red, yellow, orange to true purple. These daybloomers, growing on short, hairy tubes, last only a day or two; new flowers appear quite regularly.

Because lobivias easily propagate from seed, much hybridizing has occurred—particularly with the genera *Rebutia* and *Echinopsis*. Their free-flowering habit and compact, clustering growth form make lobivias an excellent choice for window gardens and greenhouses.

Planted in an average soil mixture and given an occasional watering, lobivias remain quite content. They should be protected from harsh, burning sun.

Lobivia famatimensis. Small globe with shallow, cross-furrowed ribs and white spines. Flowers are red or yellow, sometimes white.

L. f. densispina. Unusual variety bears 20 or more radial spines; dark green stems.

L. f. setosa. White, bristlelike radial spines; central spines are missing on this variety. Flowers are either red or yellow.

Echinopsis
Easter Lily Cactus

Height: To 1′   **Blooms:** Spring,
summer
Exposure: Sun,   **Hardiness:** 30°F.
partial shade

Heavily spined, prominent ribs and dramatic, trumpet-shaped flowers characterize the genus *Echinopsis*. These South American hedgehog cacti have been

More Echinocereus

Lobivia famatimensis

Echinopsis multiplex

Rebutia minuscula

given popular names like sea urchin and Easter lily cacti; other species are sometimes called barrel cacti. But whatever the nickname, a colorful, blooming echinopsis is very popular with experienced cactus collectors as well as beginners.

Undoubtedly, the outstanding feature is the flower. Blooms are usually 8 inches long and in shades of red, pink, or white. Most species bear nocturnally, often just for a day, though some remain open for 36 hours or more.

Cultural requirements for echinopsis are simple: a rich soil mixture (see page 75) along with ample fertilizer and water assure healthy results. Known for their hardiness, many species survive the winter in near-freezing temperatures—some even in snow. Indoors, potted echinopsis are suitable almost anywhere because they grow in areas that get either full, or partial, indirect sun.

Like many other hedgehog cacti, echinopsis propagate easily from seed and produce offsets freely. In addition, hybridizing has occurred, making immediate identification somewhat difficult. *Echinopsis* is usually confused with the genus *Lobivia,* though close examination of the flower reveals it to be larger and with a distinct circle of upper stamens at the mouth.

These are some of the most popular species available:

Echinopsis albispinosa. Gray, 6-inch stems, either single or with offsets. Curved, dark brown spines turn white at maturity. Large white flowers reach 8 inches long.

E. calochlora (SHINING BALL). Yellow radial spines, usually stout and needle-shaped, contrast against bright green stems. Small globular plant bears long, near-white flowers often bigger than itself.

E. longispina. Stout, yellowish brown spines grow from deeply undulate ribs. Flowers are many-petaled, slender, white.

E. multiplex (EASTER LILY CACTUS, BARREL CACTUS). Good choice for potted plants or grouping in landscaped areas because of impressive blooms. Long-tubed, sweetly scented, pale pink flowers can reach 10 inches long. (Photo on page 65.)

E. rhodotricha. Unusually tall for an echinopsis—may reach 2 feet or more. Curved slender spines; 6-inch-long white flowers.

E. tubiflora. Inch-long central spines are yellow with black tips; mammoth white flowers reach 4 inches wide, 10 inches long.

It is now time to relocate your plant to a warmer area and begin watering. Because they propagate easily from seeds or cuttings, much hybridizing has occurred.

From the more than 25 species of rebutias, we describe the following:

Rebutia albiflora. Tiny, almost fragile in appearance. Hairy spines, slender stems, and pure white flowers are typical of this clustering species.

R. heliosa. Densely covered with short, silvery spines. Flowers are slender, reddish orange. One of the newest rebutias to be developed.

R. kupperana. Small grayish brown globe with short brown spines and red orange flowers.

R. minuscula (RED CROWN). Clustering globular growth with bright green heads. Short white spines almost hidden by brick red flowers.

R.m. grandiflora. Similar to *R. minuscula* except that flowers appear on long, narrow tubes.

R. pseudodeminuta (WALLFLOWER CROWN). Slender spines are white with brown tips; golden yellow flowers are 2 inches long.

R. senilis (FIRE CROWN). Dark green plant covered with a mass of snow white spines; blooms profusely in brilliant red.

R. spinosissima. Close-set areoles with many bristle-like, radial white spines; delicate flowers are blood red.

Rebutia
A Hedgehog Cactus

Height: To 6″ **Blooms:** Spring, summer

Exposure: Partial shade **Hardiness:** 30°F.

When you glance 50 feet up, to the top of a giant saguaro, try to imagine the smallest member of that same family—tiny rebutias, no bigger than an apple. Though distant relatives, both *are* cacti and exemplify better than most genera the extreme diversity within a single botanical family.

Rebutias are clustering, globular cacti, originally found growing in the alpine grasses of South America. Instead of true ribs, they have small nipplelike projections. Because they bear flowers in a circle around the base, rebutias have been nicknamed crown cacti. Despite their dwarf appearance, they produce an abundance of large, highly colored blooms in red, orange, pink, yellow, purple, and white.

An average soil mixture and ample moisture during the growing season seem to be the only requirements of rebutias. They are fairly hardy in winter if kept completely dry, but do need a partially shaded location where they have protection from the sun. Early in spring you'll notice small, reddish pimples forming among the basal spines—this is the earliest indication of flowering.

From the familiar, golden-spined appearance of a barrel cactus to the curious, almost whimsical look of the living rock varieties—all are included in the next subtribe: *Echinocactanae.* Selected from it are the following genera: *Echinocactus, Gymnocalycium, Ferocactus, Astrophytum, Ariocarpus, Strombocactus, Obregonia, Notocactus,* and *Parodia.*

Echinocactus
A Barrel Cactus

Height: To 10′ **Blooms:** Spring, summer

Exposure: Sun **Hardiness:** 30°F.

Included here are the most familiar barrel sorts, recognized by their prominent ribs and heavy, colorful spination. Echinocactus are among the easiest cacti to cultivate. The free-flowering habit of mature specimens is interesting: they bear their flowers in a circle near the tender crown of the plant.

Natives to Mexico and the southwestern United States, barrel cacti are by their very nature, varied—in shape, unusual spination, and in size. Young plants make attractive container subjects, whereas older specimens are more suitable bedded outdoors. Because they can reach several feet tall and equally

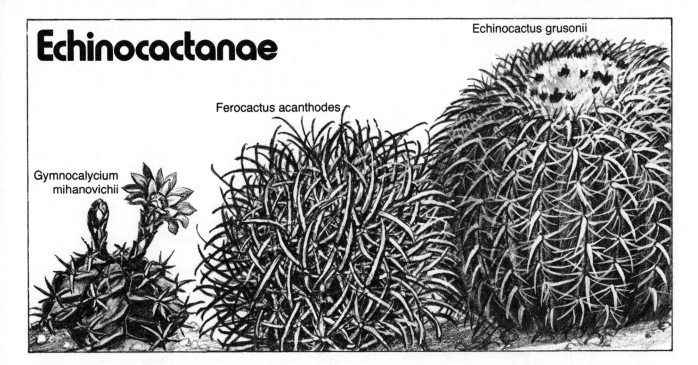

Echinocactanae

Gymnocalycium mihanovichii

Ferocactus acanthodes

Echinocactus grusonii

wide, mature echinocactus need ample room if they are displayed indoors.

They require an average soil mixture and generous but infrequent waterings, particularly during the hottest part of the summer, though their tough exterior enables them to withstand full desert conditions. In winter, they prefer cool, dry conditions and are hardy down to 30°F.

Though it may be difficult, propagation should be done by seed since echinocactus don't branch or readily produce offsets. Seeds should be sown in late spring or early summer. (For more information on propagating by seed, see page 73.)

Echinocactus grandis. Fairly large, globular shape—to 7 feet high and 3 feet thick. Straight yellowish brown spines and 1–2-inch-long yellow flowers.

E. grusonii (GOLDEN BARREL). Popularly cultivated cactus whose sharp, dark yellow spines remain colorful if grown in full sun. Bright yellow flowers, appearing on mature plants, are borne from a crown of yellow wool; they need full sunshine to remain open for any length of time. Because of their tough epidermis, golden barrels withstand full desert conditions. (Photo on page 23.)

E. horizonthalonius (EAGLE CLAWS, MULE CRIP-PLER). A native to western Texas, Arizona, New Mexico. Hard-to-find species is characterized by straight or recurved, flattened spines and a silvery gray exterior. Attractive 3-inch-long pink flowers appear in spring and summer.

E. ingens (MEXICAN GIANT BARREL). Easy to grow. Often appears in clusters, though may get as large as 3 feet thick. Straight brown spines are set off by red-centered, yellow flowers that appear in summer.

E. platyacanthus. Also known as *E. palmeri*, this un-usual variety is heavily banded with interesting purple rings when young (up to 4 inches wide).

E. polycephalus. Flattened, curved, reddish gray spines characterize this species. Flowers are 3 inches long, usually bright yellow. A native to Arizona, Nevada, Utah, even parts of southeastern California.

Ferocactus
A Barrel Cactus

Height: To 10′ **Blooms:** Spring, summer

Exposure: Sun **Hardiness:** 30°F.

Fierce-looking but fantastic, this genus is the largest of the barrel cacti, both in size and in number of varieties. Natives to much of the Southwest, ferocactus can at-tain an enormous size—up to 10 feet tall and weigh-ing hundreds of pounds. Though not known for their flowers, many produce solitary blooms at the top of their stems. Fleshy, oblong fruit has tiny black seeds.

Like many other barrel sorts, ferocactus begin as spiny globes, then broaden and become heavily ribbed. Because of their vicious-looking spination, they should be planted away from heavily traveled areas.

In winter, many species are frost resistant; most are able to withstand cool temperatures if kept completely dry.

Ferocactus acanthodes (FIRE BARREL). Cylindrical, columnar stems bear stout reddish spines. Bright yel-low flowers appear at top of stem on mature plants. Older plants have occasionally been reported to reach 9 feet tall, though most average about 4 feet. Plants have been grown as barriers against animals. (Photo on page 23.)

F. covillei (FISHHOOK CACTUS). Five-foot-high species with reddish white radial spines and solitary, hooked central spine. The nickname fishhook is often given to this vicious, central spine. Summertime flowers are red to yellow, usually 2–3 inches long.

F. glaucescens (BLUE BARREL). Solitary stem is bluish green; spines are straight and pale yellow.

F. hamatacanthus (TURK'S HEAD). Oblong stems reach 3 feet tall, are tubercled with brown spines. Yellow flowers often have red throats.

F. latispinus (DEVIL'S TONGUE CACTUS). Flat, hooked spines are yellow; central spines, red. Often single spine is deflexed, viciously protruding from center of plant. Rose-colored flowers are sweetly scented.

F. rectispinus (HATPIN CACTUS, GIANT SPINED BARREL). Incredible hatpin-sharp spines (up to 10 inches long) contrast with delightful 3-inch-long yellow flowers.

F. setispinus (STRAWBERRY CACTUS). Foot-tall stems are spiraled, deeply tubercled; spines are yellow to brown with one prominently hooked. Yellow flowers have red centers.

F. wislizenii (ARIZONA BARREL). This species has massive columnar stems with vicious, 4-inch spines. Summertime flowers are bright yellow, often marked with red at edges. Should be planted in area with open space surrounding.

Gymnocalycium
A Chin Cactus

Height: To 10″ **Blooms:** Spring, summer

Exposure: Partial shade **Hardiness:** 35°F.

Chin cacti, the nickname for gymnocalyciums, probably comes from the existence of chinlike protrusions right below each areole and spine cluster.

These globular cacti, occasionally found growing in clusters, are easily recognized by their smooth, naked flower buds and scaly fruit. Long-lasting flowers that open for several days in succession are red, pink, or white—rarely yellow. Some flowers are so small they barely appear above the curved spines of the plant.

Most gymnocalyciums prefer an average soil mixture and ample watering during the growing season. They do need protection from direct sunlight, but will tolerate cool winter temperatures if kept completely dry. Because they are among the easiest, most interesting cacti to cultivate, they're well worth the attention of beginning collectors.

From more than 80 different species, we've chosen the following:

Gymnocalycium bruchii. This plant produces large, dense clumps of bluish stems covered with bristly, white curved spines. Springtime flowers are rose-colored to white, often darker inside. (Photo on facing page.)

G. damsii. Said to be closely related to *G. schickendantzii*, though this species has all-white flowers and needlelike spines.

G. denudatum (SPIDER CACTUS). Interesting areoles and spreading, appressed, yellow spines give plant the appearance of a spider. Stems are shiny green and bulging. Pale rose or white flowers reach 3 inches across and appear freely and profusely. A native of Brazil and Argentina, this species should be given some shade during bright, warm summer months.

G. lafaldense. See *G. bruchii*.

G. mihanovichii (PLAID CACTUS). Small, gray green globe with crisscrossed ribs and curved spines. Attractive pale yellow to chartreuse flowers appear in profusion, even on young plants.

G. m. friedrichii. Dark green bodies with dark markings; some forms have pure red or yellow bodies and are known as 'Ruby Ball,' 'Blondie'. Winter requirements include a warm environment (at least 50°F.) and plenty of light. (See page 72 for a picture of grafted, red-headed gymnocalycium.)

G. multiflorum. Bright green cacti has 10-15 irregular, strongly tubercled ribs; slender, awl-shaped yellow spines. Flowers are white, pinkish, or light brown. Variety 'Albispina' has appressed, white spines.

G. oenanthemum. Dazzling but hard-to-find species has pale red, 2-inch-long flowers. Awl-shaped, recurved spines are light, tipped with darker reddish brown.

G. quehlianum (DWARF CHIN CACTUS). Beautiful, large white, red-throated flowers may appear even on young plants.

G. saglione (GIANT CHIN CACTUS). Largest of the genus, often reaching 1 foot wide. Long, thick, recurved spines are usually dark, may be reddish yellow on younger specimens. Pink or flesh-colored flowers appear at crown. (Photo on facing page.)

G. schickendantzii (WHITE CHIN CACTUS). Flattened, reddish spines turn gray with age. Flowers are white to pink, sometimes yellow.

Astrophytum
A Star Cactus

Height: To 2′ **Blooms:** Summer, autumn

Exposure: Sun, partial shade **Hardiness:** 25°F.

Bishop's cap, sea urchin cactus, sand dollar, and goat's horn cactus are various names given to different species of *Astrophytum*. These small, hemispherical cacti have only a few prominent ribs and are coated with a thin layer of white, woolly scales. Though only six different species are listed within the genus, they are curiously diverse in appearance: some are completely

Gymnocalycium bruchii

Ferocactus acanthodes (fire barrel)

Gymnocalycium saglione leutispinus

Echinocactus...

barrels are dramatically spined,
tolerant to adverse conditions

Echinocactus grusonii (golden barrel)

More Echinocactus

Astrophytum myriostigma

Ariocarpus fissuratus

A. capricorne (GOAT'S HORN CACTUS). Twisted, almost distorted spines that curl to look like the horns of a goat cover the white-flecked, globular body of this species. Thin, wavy spines seem to be woven throughout the plant, though they really come from slightly depressed areoles along the crests of the ribs. Flowers are yellow with scarlet centers.

A. myriostigma (BISHOP'S CAP). Easiest to grow but strangest to look at, bishop's cap cactus resembles a quinquesect rubber ball more than a plant. Its swollen appearance is broken by five prominent ribs, and the entire gray green body is covered with fine white wool. No spines are apparent. Its redeeming quality seems to be the ease with which it blooms—showy yellow flowers appear in summer. (Photo on page 26.)

A. ornatum (STAR CACTUS, ORNAMENTAL MONK'S HOOD). Young cacti are globular but mature ones become columnar. Both plants are heavily ribbed (usually with 8 ribs) and their bodies decorated with bands of white woolly hair. Spines are yellow but turn brown as plant ages. Like all astrophytums, this species flowers at the crown in various shades of yellow. A noted variety, 'Mirbelli', has golden spines that are somewhat shorter, less attractive.

Ariocarpus
A Living Rock Cactus

Height: To 9″   **Blooms:** Spring or autumn

Exposure: Sun, partial shade   **Hardiness:** 30°F.

Nicknamed living rocks because of their wrinkled, leathery, contorted appearance, these curious novelties camouflage themselves from natural predators by mimicking nature in the most marvelous ways. Hiding in the rocky, arid regions of Mexico and parts of Texas, they resemble fossils more than plants.

Appearing as flattened rosettes with overlapping, triangular tubercles, most ariocarpus are completely spineless, and their leathery skin is covered with raised, hornlike scales. Many species are brown or gray rather than the usual green which indicates chlorophyll. They are not only low-growing cacti but quite slow growing, as well.

A well-draining soil and infrequent waterings are vital. A thick tap root is characteristic, so repotting may be necessary more often than usual to prevent poor growth. Don't be disappointed if your plant fails to bloom—these are difficult cacti to raise and are temperamental when it comes to flowering.

Though no ariocarpus can be described as dull, here are a few of the truly unique ones:

Ariocarpus agavoides. Long, leathery tubercles are greenish brown and flat. Sand and dirt collect on these tubercles and help plant achieve a well-disguised look. Daytime flowers are deep magenta and appear (if they want to) on mature plants in late autumn.

spineless, while others produce dense, woolly hair; all are free-flowering with attractive, slightly scented yellow or red blooms. Single flowers—sometimes two or more grouped together—open on successive days and crown the cap of the cactus with color.

Astrophytums prefer a slightly sandy soil (see page 75 for soil mixes) and less than average amounts of water. Propagation is best handled by seed or by grafting. Most plants can withstand full sun, but partial shade is best during hottest months.

Because of their compact size and unique appearance, they are highly regarded specimens and many collectors use their limited greenhouse space to display only astrophytums.

Astrophytum asterias (SEA URCHIN CACTUS, SAND DOLLAR). Appropriately nicknamed, this species, with its flattened globular body and spineless, prominent ribs curiously resembles something from the Deep. Large, white, pimplelike areoles dot the gray green surface of the cactus. Yellow flowers with contrasting scarlet throats appear in summer.

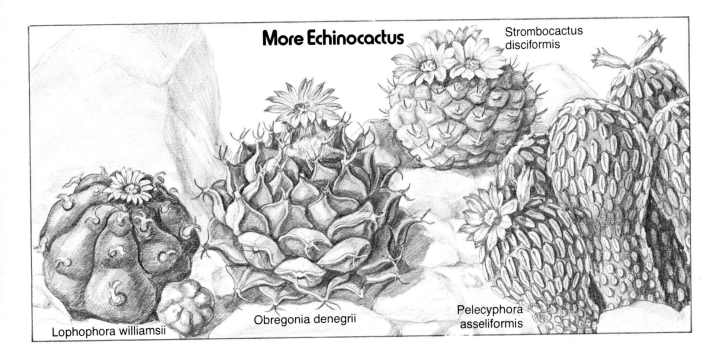

More Echinocactus

Strombocactus disciformis

Lophophora williamsii

Obregonia denegrii

Pelecyphora asseliformis

A. fissuratus (LIVING ROCK, STAR CACTUS). Flattened globe of spreading, dirty green tubercles resembles a weathered rock more than a cactus. The top surface is furrowed or grooved, parallel to the outer edges of the plant. Rose pink flowers may appear in spring.

A. kotschubeyanus. Pointed, flat tubercles covered with wool create a pattern. *A. k. macdowellii* has deep magenta to purple flowers, 1 inch wide.

A. retusus (SEVEN STARS). Three-sided tubercles form a triangular rosette. Surface is quite wrinkled, grayish brown, and slightly concave. Flowers are white, occasionally trimmed in pink.

A. scapharostrus. Rarest species. Similar to *A. agavoides* except tubercles are more erect.

A. trigonus. Largest species in size, reaching 9–12 inches across in a few cases. Tubercles are greenish gray, shriveled, and form an elongated pyramid, giving a stacked appearance. Two-inch flowers are yellow or dark cream-colored.

Other living rocks

Similar both in appearance and culture, the following living rock cacti are listed as a group rather than under each specific genera.

From the dozens of collected species and varieties, we have chosen these:

Aztekium ritteri. A Mexican native, this small, flattened, globular cactus is distinguished by its low, 3-edged, cross-furrowing ribs. Areoles form a woolly midline on each main rib. The depressed crown produces thick spines; but as plant ages, spines fall off. Flowers are white and very small—about ½-inch wide.

Lophophora williamsii (PEYOTE). Though not really a living rock in the true sense, this interesting species— better known to some as peyote—is customarily categorized here. Its spineless, blue green body has a flattened crown and a body that tapers into a thick tap root. Older specimens have transversely furrowed tubercles and areoles that bear tufts of fine hair. Flowers are pale pink, rarely white.

Though considered a sacred plant to many Indians of North America, this cactus is viewed differently by the United States Government. Restrictions on selling and transporting (to say nothing of chewing) *Lophophora williamsii* are strongly enforced because of its hallucinogenic effect when consumed.

Obregonia denegrii. Rosette of leaflike tubercles top this turnip-shaped cactus. White flowers and fruit, though hidden among white wool, peak out from cactus' crown. Spines are curved and small. Overall appearance of this species resembles a squashed pine cone.

Pelecyphora asseliformis (HATCHET CACTUS). Dark gray green, hatchet-shaped tubercles do not overlap like other species. Tiny spines (about ¼-inch long) are flat, barely visible. Flowers are deep rose. A very slow-growing plant.

Pelecyphora strobiliformis (*Encephalocarpus strobiliformis*) (PINE CONE CACTUS). Plant is not typically flattened but globular, resembling cone scales from a pine tree. Areoles, appearing at tips of tubercles, produce long spines. Flowers are rose-colored or magenta.

Strombocactus disciformis. Partially globose body—about 3 inches thick—is covered with ¾-inch-wide tubercles that are curved upward and slightly "winged" looking. From the center of the crown come white or cream-colored flowers.

Astrophytum myriostigma (bishop's cap)

Parodia aureispina
(Tom Thumb)

More Echinocactus...
ball and star-shaped species

Notocactus brevihamata

Notocactus
leninghausii

Parodia
mutabilis

N. scopa

Notocactus
A Ball Cactus

Height: To 2′ **Blooms:** Spring, summer

Exposure: Sun **Hardiness:** 30°F.

Lovely to look at and easy to grow—what better reasons could anyone have for selecting a notocactus or two. These small, ball cacti from South America are excellent potted plants for the beginner. Their simple cultural requirements and fascinating appearance—wait until you see the colorful spination—make them exciting additions to anyone's collection.

From more than 20 species, we selected these:

Notocactus apricus (SUN CUP). This 3-inch-wide species produces yellow radial spines that colorfully contrast with curved, reddish, central ones. Yellow flowers appear on 3-inch-long stout tubes from the crown.

N. brevihamata (Also sold as *Parodia brevihamata*). Newly grown species with golden yellow flowers. (Photo on opposite page.)

N. haselbergii (SCARLET BALL). Soft white spines cover this early spring-blooming species. Small, reddish orange flowers are long lasting, sometimes up to 4 weeks.

N. leninghausii (GOLDEN BALL). One of the largest ball cacti, this species produces 30 or more ribs and reaches 3 feet tall. Its shape often becomes elongated and cylindrical with age, and the top appears to tilt to one side. Large yellow flowers (on mature plants only) are long lasting.

N. ottonis (INDIAN HEAD). Clustering, globular plant with bristly, reddish brown spines and bright yellow flowers. A widely cultivated species, its many varieties include 'Tenuispinus' and 'Longispinus'.

N. scopa (SILVER BALL). Globular, heavily ribbed ball covered with silvery white, soft spines. Two-inch-wide, deep yellow flowers.

Parodia
A Ball Cactus

Height: To 10″ **Blooms:** Summer

Exposure: Sun, partial shade **Hardiness:** 30°F.

The parodias are a delightful group of small, solitary plants known for their hooked spines and clustering, colorful blooms. Similar in appearance to notocactus, parodias are free-flowering, offering summertime blooms in all shades of red, yellow, and orange. Their compact, almost hemispherical shape makes them ideal plants for dish gardens, windowsills, lath houses, and greenhouses.

Parodias grow well in an average, fast-draining soil mix and need generous, fairly frequent waterings during the growing season. They are sensitive to cold winter temperatures, preferring a protected spot where they can have an annual rest.

Parodia aureispina (TOM THUMB). Tiny, bright green spherical body has hooked, golden spines and large yellow orange flowers. (Photo on facing page.)

P. mutabilis. Fast-growing, early-blooming species has yellow flowers, often with red throats. Central spines are interesting—needle sharp, hooked, and red.

P. sanguiniflora (CRIMSON PARODIA). Dazzling, large red flowers appear in summer. Spiral, hooked, central spines are reddish brown.

Hylocereanae

Aporocactus flagelliformis

Hylocereus undatus

native to tropic areas of Central and South America, they require a rich soil and abundant watering, as well as temperatures of 50°F. or higher. They thrive in warm winter areas when bedded in partial shade.

Hylocereus minutiflorus. Three-angled, almost cylindrical stems are bright green. Fragrant, 2-inch-long flowers are white and may remain open in early morning.

H. undatus (NIGHT BLOOMING CEREUS, QUEEN OF THE NIGHT, HONOLULU QUEEN). In tropic regions, grown as hedges, but will become epiphytic climber (tree dweller) if left alone. This easy-to-grow species has bright green, branched stems that are 3-angled and have horny projections. Enormous white flowers—some reach an incredible 14 inches long—offer a subtle, nocturnal fragrance.

Aporocactus
A Climbing Cactus

Height: To 3'
Exposure: Sun, partial shade
Blooms: Spring
Hardiness: 45°F.

Free-flowering, long-stemmed plants, nicknamed rat's tails, are another of the climbing cacti. In their native habitat, they can be found hanging from trees or rocks; in cultivation, aporocactus make fine basket plants—their dangling stems cascade down 3 feet or more. (An unusual species of a climbing cactus, *Hildawinteria aureispina,* is shown on page 50.)

Aporocactus flagelliformis (RAT'S TAIL CACTUS). Hanging pot favorite. Narrow stems—resembling cat's tails rather than rat's—cascade over edge. Stems have 8–12 ribs that are completely covered with tiny, reddish brown spines. Funnel-shaped, red, spring flowers.

Selenicereus
A Climbing Cactus

Height: To 15'
Exposure: Sun, partial shade
Blooms: Spring
Hardiness: 40°F.

Night-blooming cereus is the common name most often used for the genus *Selenicereus,* though some still prefer to use moon cactus. In either case, the plants were undoubtedly named for their spectacular, nocturnal flowers. Dull green, almost spineless stems produce a vinelike growth; super-sized, white flowers.

Selenicereus grandiflorus. Hard-to-find species; much hybridizing has occurred. 'Tellii' and 'Armatus' are cultivars.

S. macdonaldiae (QUEEN OF THE NIGHT). Foot-long, yellowish white flowers grow from 5-angled stems.

S. pteranthus (PRINCESS OF THE NIGHT). Flowers smaller than queen mother *(S. macdonaldiae),* though just as pretty.

Some crawl, others can climb, but all like to cling to something. That's a silly but accurate description of the tropical subtribe *Hylocereanae,* whose aerial roots attach themselves to almost anything.

Hylocereus
A Climbing Cactus

Height: To 6'
Exposure: Partial shade
Blooms: Summer
Hardiness: 50°F.

Enormous, dazzling flowers grow from 3-angled or "winged" stems on this tropical climbing cactus. Their stems are so weak and thin that most species use their aerial roots to latch onto surrounding rocks, trees, fence posts—just about anything.

Magnificent, nocturnal flowers, usually white but sometimes red or pink, open on successive nights during the late spring or summer. Because they all are

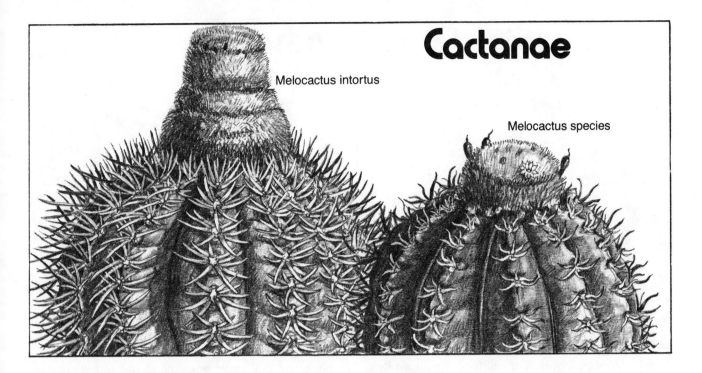

Melocactus intortus

Melocactus species

Cactanae

The subtribe *Cactanae* has two tropical genera, *Melocactus* and *Discocactus*, that have something in common: a top hat. When young, both look like most other globular cacti—round, heavy ribbed with attractive spination. As they reach maturity and get ready to flower for the first time, something unique happens. A *cephalium* or mass of bristles and wool develops at the crown of the plant. Often, it is a contrasting color—reddish brown on some species, yellow on others; in both genera, these striking *cephalia* forms are highlighted further with the appearance of colorful flowers.

Melocactus
A Melon Cactus

Height: To 4′ **Blooms:** Summer
Exposure: Sun **Hardiness:** 50°F.

Exotic, fascinating, but temperamental genus that is best left for the more experienced cactus enthusiast.

One of the oldest known cacti—early explorers in the 1500s returned to Europe with melocactus—but also one of the hardest to raise because of their demanding cultural requirements.

Melocactus can only survive in a greenhouse where the temperature doesn't fall below 50°F. They need a porous, rich soil that offers perfect drainage, modest amounts of water, and sufficient heat and light even during the winter months. It is almost impossible to provide enough room for optimum growth because of their shallow but extremely spreading root system.

Melocactus communis (TURK'S CAP, MELON CACTUS). Three-foot-tall cactus with a low (2-inch) cephalium. Yellowish spines, red or pinkish flowers.

M. intortus (TURK'S CAP CACTUS). Largest species—cactus body reaches 3 feet high and cephalium, 1 foot above that. Spines are reddish brown, about 1 inch long; daytime flowers are pink.

M. neryi. If there is such a thing as an easy-to-grow melocactus, this is it. Cultural requirements seem less demanding. Small, 6-inch body is topped with 4-inch cephalium. Inch-long flowers are rosy pink.

M. oaxacensis. Smallest, often rarest melocactus. Stems are about 6 inches thick, no more than 10 inches high. Cephalium is reddish brown but turns gray; blooms are very dark rose.

Discocactus
A Melon Cactus

Height: To 6″ **Blooms:** Summer
Exposure: Sun **Hardiness:** 55°F.

Discocactus, one of the toughest plants to raise—let alone obtain—offers the ultimate challenge to any cactus grower. Native to South America, they typically are small, solitary bodies with many ribs, thick spines, and large, nocturnal flowers. Like melocactus, these plants require the consistently steady environment of a warm, well-lighted greenhouse, as well as rich, fast-draining soil.

Discocactus alteolens. Large, fragrant white flowers appear on this species at dusk but by morning are gone. Mature plant stands 4 inches high, including cephalium. Woolly mass is dark gray, almost black but turns lighter with age.

D. placentiformis. Five-inch-high cactus has flattened, curved spines and slender, tubular pink flowers.

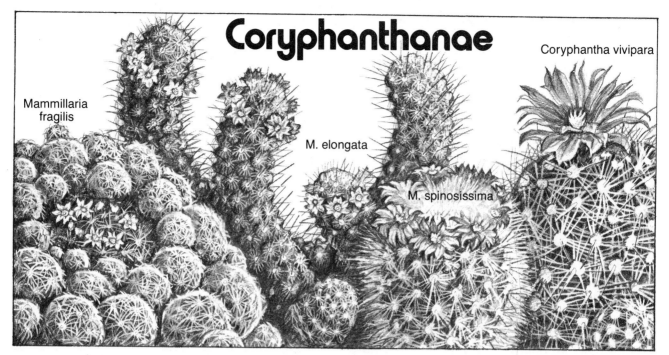

Coryphanthanae

Mammillaria fragilis

M. elongata

M. spinosissima

Coryphantha vivipara

Ruby dumpling, golf ball cactus, little candles, powder puff, thimble cactus, and much more—these are just a few delightfully descriptive common names from *Coryphanthanae*. Though there are probably 15 or so genera within this group, *Coryphantha* and *Mammillaria* are unquestionably the two most often mentioned.

Because they both have lines of nipplelike tubercles over their entire body (not just on the stems) and are void of any true ribs, the two appear quite similar. Both like an average, porous soil mixture, bright light (not scorching direct sunlight) to encourage flowering, and frequent, generous waterings during the growing season.

Unfortunately, there are over 400 different *Mammillaria* and *Coryphantha* species; we obviously must limit our selection to just a few. We've chosen the following ones because they are the most popular and easily obtainable, and least demanding species.

Mammillaria
A Pincushion Cactus

Height: To 1′

Blooms: Spring, summer

Exposure: Sun, partial shade

Hardiness: 35°F.

The seemingly endless variety of shapes, sizes, and colors is apparent in the more than 350 species of *Mammillaria*. They can be solitary plants or clustering groups, spined with soft bristles or thorny hooks, and crowned with a few single flowers or a circle of delicate blooms.

Though diverse in appearance, their culture remains the same: an average or slightly sandy soil mixture,

infrequent but ample amounts of water, and sufficient bright light to be profusely covered with blooms each year. "Mamms" are extremely easy to grow, and their dwarf, compact size makes them suitable potted plants for lath houses and greenhouses, windowsills, tabletop displays or dish gardens.

Mammillaria bocasana (POWDER PUFF). Clustering growth forms cushionlike habit. Globular, with snow white silky hairs and yellow flowers. Hooked central spine is also yellow, points downward and out. Easily raised from seed.

M. bombycina (SILK PINCUSHION). Free-flowering species produces red flowers in garlandlike circle at crown. Silky white radial spines contrast with darker central ones. Plant changes from globular to cylindrical with age.

M. candida (SNOWBALL PINCUSHION). Spreading, white bristly spines have brown tips. Flattened, spherical body is densely covered with short spines that often hide ½-inch pink flowers.

***M. compressa*.** Clumping species, often to 3 feet wide, has gray green body covered with short, milky tubercles. Spreading, needle-shaped spines are white; one is curved downward. Purple red flowers appear in spring.

M. comptotricha (BIRD'S NEST CACTUS). Tiny white flowers are barely noticed except for their sweet, lime scent. Plant clusters but has a tangled, messy appearance.

***M. confusa*.** Globular to clustering plant has interesting spiral configuration of tubercles; woolly white bristles contrast with dark radial spines. Blooms, if any, are greenish white and appear in spring or summer.

***M. elegans*.** Six-inch-high cluster has spiral tubercles and white, needle-shaped radial spines. Central spines

Mammillaria tetrancistra

Mammillaria guerreronis

Mammillaria...

a garland of flowers surrounds each crown

Mammillaria elongata 'Pink Nymph'

Mammillaria spinosissima (red-headed Irishman)

are thicker, black-tipped; scarlet flowers in spring.

M. elongata (LACE CACTUS, GOLDEN STAR). Creamy yellow flowers, only ½ inch wide, appear in spring. Columnar body has slightly spreading, yellow-colored spination; tends to branch from the base. Cultivars: 'Longispina,' 'Rufocrocea.' (Photo on page 31.)

M. fragilis (THIMBLE CACTUS). Delicate, miniature species appears to have tiny plants growing from the top of its cylindrical, cepitose body. Brown-tipped, white central spines grow outward. Pale yellow flowers are only ½ inch long.

M. geminispina. Clumping stems to 8 inches tall have many curving bristles. Two central spines—one directed upward, the other down—are white with brown tips. Flowers are carmine, often striped with white.

M. guerreronis. Clustering, somewhat elongated stems may reach 2 feet tall. Needle-shaped, pure white spines highlight edges. (Photo on page 31.)

M. hahniana (OLD LADY CACTUS, OLD LADY OF MEXICO). Gray green body produces slender, white radial spines that appear to overlap. Purplish red to pink blooms, sometimes to 1 inch wide, appear in summer. Long, white flowing hair covers plant to resemble head of elderly person.

M. heyderi (CORAL CACTUS). Simple, hemispheric shape to 6 inches wide; brown-tipped, white radial spines are directed outward. Extremely prolific bloomer. Flowers, 1–1½ inches long, are white, sometimes tinged with pink or red at edges. Also sold as M. gummifera.

M. kewensis. Purple flowers appear throughout summer on this species. Thick, needle-shaped spines change from light to dark with age.

M. longimamma. Pale yellow spines turn dark brown; magnificent 3-inch-long flowers in shades of yellow appear in summer. One of the easiest mammillarias to get to flower at an early age.

M. parksonii (OWL'S EYE). Young growth is globular, then branches and forms clumps. Stems are covered with white, miniscule spines. Pink-tinged white flowers appear in summer.

M. plumosa (FEATHER CACTUS). Clumping, 3-inch-wide plant is completely covered with soft white spines. Greenish white flowers rarely are seen in cultivation.

M. prolifera (LITTLE CANDLES). In spring, profusely covered with small, funnel-shaped, pale yellow flowers. Clumping plant produces tiny offsets and attractive, though few-seeded, red fruit.

M. spinosissima (RED-HEADED IRISHMAN). Long, cylindrical body, to 1 foot tall, is densely covered with interlacing, white spines. Crown is covered with circle of small, reddish purple flowers. (Photo on page 31.)

M. tetrancistra. Rose purple flowers contrast with dark, hooked spines. Sometimes called fishhook cactus. (Photo on page 31.)

M. wildii (FISHHOOK PINCUSHION). Clumping plant grows to 6 inches tall, may branch at base to form clustering groups. Short bristles, borne from areoles, are white. A circle of flowers, usually white or tinted with red or pink, appears at the crown in summer.

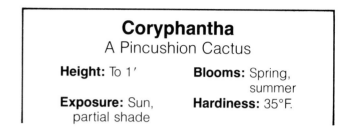

Coryphantha
A Pincushion Cactus

Height: To 1′

Blooms: Spring, summer

Exposure: Sun, partial shade

Hardiness: 35°F.

A quick glance at the genus Coryphantha suggests a striking resemblance to most mammillarias. Their appearance differs slightly, though, in two ways: instead of the typical globular growth as in mammillarias, coryphanthas also cluster in large mounds or become columnar with age. Also, coryphanthas have only one kind of areole—flowers and spiny areas are joined by a woolly groove.

Because most of the subtribe Coryphanthanae are easy to grow and readily available, cactus enthusiasts have been known to limit their collections to just these specialties. The genus Coryphantha, whose original habitat was Mexico and parts of the Southwest, has 66 species alone. All are free-flowering, producing large, showy flowers (1–3 inches long) in spring or summer. Red, yellow, or purple blooms are most common, though rare species bear white ones.

These species are among the most popular coryphanthas:

Coryphantha cornifera. Five-inch-high, globular plant has interesting, spirally configured tubercles; yellow spines turn gray with age. Yellow flowers are 2 inches long, appear in summer.

C. macromeris (DONNA ANNA CACTUS). Species characterized by clustering, 5-inch stems and loose tubercles. Radial spines are white, needle-shaped; centrals are shorter, darker. Summertime blooms are large—up to 3 inches long—and purple.

C. missouriensis. Small species, usually under 3 inches high, has stout spines, one of which is long and directed outward. Greenish yellow, fragrant flowers.

C. scheeri. Beautiful spination—radial spines are yellow tipped with red. Showy flowers, either plain yellow or streaked with red or pink, reach 3 inches wide.

C. strobiliformis. Compact, 5-inch-high species has bright pink or purple flowers. C. s. durispina and C. s. orcutti are recognized varieties.

C. vivipara. Probably the best-known species. Slightly depressed, globular plant has unique spination: the central spine is directed outward, the others down. C. v. alversonii reaches 6 inches high and branches; C. v. bisbeeana (GOLF BALL CACTUS) will form mounds or be slightly branched. Both have pink flowers about 1½ inches wide.

1 cotton ball and 2 eagle claws

Though delightfully descriptive, common names are not too dependable. See what happens when you go into a nursery asking for a Honolulu queen or a Mexican mule crippler—you may get nothing more than a hearty laugh, or at best, a confused stare. Don't expect a nurseryworker to come up with the right plant. Not only are common names rarely used, but they vary according to geographic location and the particular grower. Nurseries know that the only way to be accurate is to label plants with their botanical names.

Our list is merely a chance to see all the common names of cacti together. It may help you learn to identify them more easily because in most cases they're accurately descriptive—just take a look at bishop's cap (*Astrophytum myriostigma*) or bunny ears (*Opuntia microdasys*) or woolly torch (*Cephalocereus palmeri*) and you'll see what we mean.

Beaver tail (*Opuntia basilaris*)
Bird's nest cactus (*Mammillaria camptotricha*)
Bishop's cap (*Astrophytum myriostigma*)
Blue barrel (*Ferocactus glaucescens*)
Bunny ears (*Opuntia microdasys*)

Christmas cactus (*Schlumbergera bridgesii*)
Coral cactus (*Mammillaria heyderi*)
Cotton ball (*Espostoa lanata*)
Crimson parodia (*Parodia sanguiniflora*)
Curiosity plant (*Cereus peruvianus* 'Monstrosus')

Dagger cactus (*Lemaireocereus gummosus*)
Devil's tongue cactus (*Ferocactus latispinus*)
Dutchman's pipe (*Epiphyllum oxypetalum*)
Dwarf chin cactus (*Gymnocalycium quehlianum*)

Eagle claws (*Echinocactus horizonthalonius*)
Easter lily cactus (*Echinopsis multiplex*)
Elephant cactus (*Pachycereus pringlei*)

Feather cactus (*Mammillaria plumosa*)
Fire crown (*Rebutia senilis*)
Fishbone cactus (*Epiphyllum anguliger*)
Fishhook cactus (*Ferocactus wislizensii*)
Fishhook pincushion (*Mammillaria wildii*)

Giant chin cactus (*Gymnocalycium saglione*)
Goat's horn cactus (*Astrophytum capricorne*)
Golden ball (*Notocactus leninghausii*)
Golden barrel (*Echinocactus grusonii*)
Golden spines (*Cephalocereus chrysacanthus*)
Golden star (*Mammillaria elongata*)
Golden torch (*Trichocereus spachianus*)
Golf ball cactus (*Coryphantha vivipara bisbeeana*)

Hatchet cactus (*Pelecyphora asselliformis*)
Hatpin cactus (*Ferocactus rectispinus*)
Hedgehog cactus—name for genus *ECHINOCEREUS*
Honolulu queen (*Hylocereus undatus*)

Indian comb (*Pachycereus pecten-aboriginum*)
Indian fig (*Opuntia ficus-indica*)
Indian head (*Notocactus ottonis*)

Joseph's coat (*Opuntia vulgaris* 'Variegata')
Jumping cholla (*Opuntia prolifera*)

Lace cactus (*Echinocereus reichenbachii*)
Link plant (*Rhipsalis paradoxa*)
Little candles (*Mammillaria prolifera*)
Living rocks—name for genus *ARIOCARPUS*

Mexican giant (*Cephalocereus fulviceps*)
Mexican giant barrel (*Echinocactus ingens*)
Mistletoe cactus (*Rhipsalis baccifera*)
Mule crippler (*Echinocactus horizonthalonius*)

Night-blooming cereus (*Hylocereus undatus*)

Old lady cactus (*Mammillaria hahniana*)
Old man cactus (*Cephalocereus senilis*)
Orchid cactus—name for genus *EPIPHYLLUM*
Organ pipe cactus (*Lemaireocereus marginatus* OR
   L. thurberi)
Owl's eye (*Mammillaria parksonii*)

Paraguay ball (*Notocactus schumannianus*)
Peanut cactus (*Chamacereus sylvestrii*)
Peruvian apple (*Cereus peruvianus*)
Peruvian torch (*Trichocereus peruvianus*)
Peyote (*Lophophora williamsii*)
Pine cone cactus (*Pelecyphora strobiliformis*)
Plaid cactus (*Gymnocalycium mihanovichii*)
Polka dot (*Opuntia microdasys* 'Albispina')
Powder puff (*Mammillaria bocasana*)
Princess of the night (*Selenicereus pteranthus*)

Queen of the night (*Selenicereus macdonaldiae*)

Rainbow cactus (*Echinocereus pectinatus
   rigidissimus* OR *E.p. neomexicanus*)
Rat's tail cactus (*Aporocactus flagelliformis*)

Saguaro (*Carnegeia gigantea*)
Sand dollar (*Astrophytum asterias*)
Scarlet ball (*Notocactus haselbergii*)
Scarlet bugler (*Cleistocactus baumanii*)
Sea urchin cactus—name for genus *ASTROPHYTUM*
Seven stars (*Ariocarpus retusus*)
Shining ball (*Echinopsis calochlora*)
Silk pincushion (*Mammillaria bombycina*)
Silver ball (*Notocactus scopa*)
Silver torch (*Cleistocactus straussii*)
Snowball pincushion (*Mammillaria candida*)
Spider cactus (*Gymnocalycium denudatum*)
Star cactus (*Astrophytum ornatum*)
Strawberry cactus (*Echinocereus enneacanthus* OR
   Ferocactus setispinus)
Sun cactus (*Heliocereus speciosus*)
Sun cup (*Notocactus apricus*)

Teddy bear cactus (*Opuntia bigelovii*)
Thimble cactus (*Mammillaria fragilis*)
Tom Thumb (*Parodia aureispina*)
Toothpick cactus (*Stetsonia coryne*)
Turk's cap (*Melocactus intortus*)
Turk's head (*Ferocactus hamatacanthus*)

Wallflower crown (*Rebutia pseudodeminuta*)
Whisker cactus (*Lophocereus schottii*)
White chin cactus (*Gymnocalycium schickendantzii*)
Woolly torch (*Cephalocereus palmeri*)

Epiphyllum hybrid

Epiphyllum hybrid 'Cinco de Mayo'

Epiphyllum...
fleshy stems, brilliant flowers

Epiphyllum hybrids:
(clockwise from top) 'Fifi', 'King Midas', 'Concerto', 'Clara Ann'

Epiphytes

Epiphyllum hybrid

Rhipsalidopsis gaertneri

Rhipsalis species

Epiphyllums are easy to grow. They can be left alone to grow in a pendantlike habit, or staked on a trellis or some other support. Give them bright, filtered light and a porous, sandy soil. Since they do best when their roots are crowded, pot them in small containers. Let them dry out between waterings; they thrive in cool night temperatures (50°F.). In winter, rest the plants and keep the soil just barely moist. If possible, locate epiphyllums in an unheated (but not freezing) garage or porch.

When they are blooming, usually in May or June, enjoy them both indoors and out. A prolific bloomer is assured if you give it plenty of light—without it, plants never reach their flowering potential.

Some of the widely cultivated species include *Epiphyllum anguliger* (FISHBONE CACTUS), *E. oxypetalum* (DUTCHMAN'S PIPE), and *E. strictum.*

Rhipsalis
An Epiphytic Cactus

Height: To 10′
Exposure: Partial shade

Blooms: Winter
Hardiness: 50°F.

Resembling and consequently nicknamed coral cactus, rhipsalis have a unique branching habit: some species have thin, crisscrossing stems that weave in and out of each other. This interesting, cascading growth makes rhipsalis an attractive hanging plant. Flowers are insignificantly small, appear in winter rather than summer, and are not considered especially beautiful. Most flowers are red, white, or yellow, occasionally with streaked throats or edges.

Like other epiphytic plants, rhipsalis thrive in temperatures of 55°F. or more, though night temperatures can fall to 45°F. if plant is thoroughly protected. They should be rested for 6–8 weeks each fall; keep the soil just barely moist. Propagation can be done by cuttings or, when available, by seed.

Some popular rhipsalis are: *Rhipsalis baccifera* (MISTLETOE CACTUS), *R. cereuscula* (CORAL CACTUS, POPCORN), *R. paradoxa* (LINK CACTUS), and *R. warmingiana.*

Epiphytes, or tree dwellers, are cacti from the tropical jungles of Central and South America and parts of Mexico. Growing on the bark or branches of trees, these plants gather nourishment from surrounding moss, leaf mold, or other debris.

Epiphyllum
An Epiphytic Cactus

Height: To 10′

Exposure: Partial sun

Blooms: Spring, summer
Hardiness: 50°F.

Epiphyllum hybrids, relatives of the rain forest species of the Tropics, are spineless plants with flattened, scallop-edged stems and enormous flowers. Nowhere else in the Cactus family has such progress been made by hybridizers to achieve mammoth flowers in so many brilliant colors—over 3,000 named hybrids exist.

Other epiphytes

Similar to epiphyllums—except that flowers appear at the tips of the stems, not from the sides—are the species of *Schlumbergera.* Nicknamed Christmas cactus *(S. bridgesii)* and Thanksgiving cactus *(S. truncata)* because flowers appear in late autumn and winter, these epiphytes rank among the most popular flowering house plants.

Rhipsalidopsis, another tropical cactus, has flattened upper joints and shorter, lower ones. Flowers are larger than those of *Rhipsalis;* cultural requirements are the same. The most cultivated species, *Rhipsalidopsis gaertneri* (EASTER CACTUS) produces bright red flowers (2–3 inches wide) in spring.

Favorite Succulents

Just like their spiny cactus cousins, the succulent families are an irresistible group. Particularly fascinating for many people, they have long been prized for their distinctive foliage, beautiful flowers, and interesting forms. More often than not, these three traits are handsomely combined in a single plant.

Simple-to-grow succulents

With little exception, succulents are simple to grow. Though they come from different habitats (this usually gives an indication as to growing demands later on), they can live in remarkably similar environments. In lath houses and greenhouses, indoors and out, succulent plants are one of the hardiest, most adaptive groups around.

Most species enjoy the advantage of a well-lighted location, which usually brings out their intense foliage color. Flowers are more prolific, too, when sufficient light is provided. A well-drained potting mix (soggy soil can be lethal) that gets generous but infrequent amounts of water is best for succulent plants. During winter, water more sparingly.

Good circulation of clean, fresh air is also essential. A stuffy atmosphere, whether indoors or in a greenhouse, will prevent healthy growth, so check to see that adequate ventilation is provided as much as possible. Winter temperatures should also be watched. (See individual plant listings for varying degrees of hardiness.)

Choose from dozens and dozens

The dozens of forms and colorful varieties open a world of beautiful plants to the succulent gardener. *Cotyledon undulata* resembles a pale green, delicately carved piece of porcelain. Some euphorbias, with their bizarre, contorted shapes, look like they just exploded. The handsomely mottled foliage of a few kalanchoes and gasterias make them popular, while other species, like bold-leafed aloes and agaves, look more like pieces of sculpture than plants.

Among the succulents good for container life, the jade plant *(Crassula argentea)* and the donkey tail *(Sedum morganianum)* are indestructible, popular house plants. Somehow, they manage in locations where everything else has failed. Crown-of-thorns *(Euphorbia milii)*, poinsettias *(E. pulcherrima)*, and colorful kalanchoes have withstood the test of time as beautiful gift plants. And the familiar wax plant *(Hoya carnosa)* and rosary vine *(Ceropegia woodii)* offer the perfect solution for suspending plants in out-of-the-way corners from patio overhangs; their trailing habit cascades down in graceful forms.

Though many succulents make great container plants, indoors and out, nowhere do they display their versatility better than when featured in landscapes. Prolific crassulas and even the tiniest sedums thrive in shady beds or in rock crevices filled with soil. When two or three species are planted together, they create a living tapestry that combines with other surroundings. Larger species—boldly-formed euphorbias and wide-leafed agaves—become the backbone of permanent land-

scapes, while creeping succulents, like various ice plants and other dependable mesembryanthemums, carpet an entire area with solid color.

Over rocks, around the base of trees, down hillsides, or in a bed—succulent plants are dependably hard working yet dramatically showy. When soil is poor or it is too shady for annuals, THINK SUCCULENTS. When the hill is so steep that everything fails (or simply washes away), THINK SUCCULENTS. When temperatures fluctuate to threatening extremes, THINK SUCCULENTS. And when rains fail to come and nothing seems to survive, THINK SUCCULENTS. They are the least demanding, most versatile group of plants we know.

Introducing...

So far, you've met only one group of succulents—CACTUS. Now it is time to introduce the rest of the families in the succulent community. Meet: The euphorbias, the crassulas, the milkweeds, the lilies, the agaves, the daisies, and the mesembryanthemums.

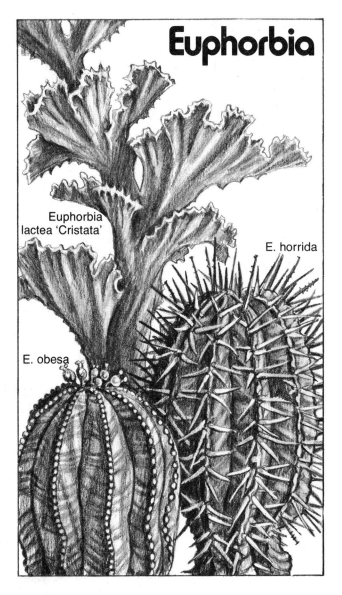

Euphorbia

Euphorbia
lactea 'Cristata'

E. horrida

E. obesa

same decorative function as sculpture. They are striking in form, attractive in texture and color, slow-growing enough to stay in scale with their surroundings, and reasonably tolerant of dry indoor air.

Euphorbia aggregata. Cactus-shaped succulent with colorful red spines. (Photo on facing page.)

E. bupleurifolia (PINEAPPLE EUPHORBIA). Fascinating oddity because of its thick stems which are covered with brown scalelike tubercles. Overall appearance is that of a pineapple or pine cone. In spring, light green leaves appear and remain until winter. (Photo on facing page.)

E. canariensis. Candelabra succulent that reaches treelike stature. (Photo on facing page.)

E. caput-medusae (MEDUSA'S HEAD). Serpentinelike branches, about 2 feet long, grow out of partially buried, globose crown. Cuttings can be rooted easily but may fail to produce symmetrically branched plants.

E. cereiformis (MILK BARREL). Spiny, succulent shrubs reach 3 feet tall. Solitary, reddish brown spines turn gray with age. Thick, dark green ribs have spiral or twisted appearance.

E. grandicornis (COW'S HORN). A decorative plant with whorling branches, growing in tiers. Stems are ribbed, divided into segments; individual ribs have wavelike spination.

E. grandidens (BIG TOOTH EUPHORBIA). Though mature specimens reach 30 feet in native habitats, potted subjects remain small, attractive for years. Branches arise in whorls from main stem.

E. horrida (AFRICAN MILK BARREL). Ferociously armed with thorns, this species resembles a barrel cactus with ribs and toothed crests. Reasonably tough plant that withstands some neglect.

E. ingens. Candelabra-type growth; stems have dark green wavy ribs.

E. lactea (MOTTLED SPURGE, DRAGON BONES). Spiny shrub with candelabra-shaped growth has dark green stems that are edged in white. Pairs of dark brown spines appear on the ridges. *E. l.* 'Cristata' (ELK'S HORN) has crested, distorted branches.

E. mammillaris (CORKSCREW). A low plant with cylindrical, ribbed stems; looks like a cactus.

E. milii (CROWN OF THORNS, CHRIST PLANT). Bright green leaves and vibrant scarlet flowers (yellow to cream on hybrids); woody stems. (Photo on facing page.)

E. obesa (BASEBALL PLANT). Perfectly shaped round ball; gray green epidermis with purple markings. Completely spineless, tiny tubercles.

E. pulcherrima (POINSETTIA). Well-known Christmas plant whose flowers (actually leaf bracts) are red, pink, or white.

E. trigona (AFRICAN MILK TREE, ABYSSINIAN EUPHORBIA). Fast-growing species has dark green stems with contrasting, wavy white bands down the sides.

Looking at the sharply armed crown of thorns (Euphorbia milii), you'd never guess it belongs to the same family as the lovely poinsettia (E. pulcherrima). The Euphorbia family, sometimes called the "spurge family," has over 200 different genera. In fact, there are about 1,000 species in the genus Euphorbia alone. Some of them—especially the columnar and tree types—resemble cactus; others are dwarf species or globe-shaped plants. Except for a few varieties, euphorbias bear only small, insignificant flowers.

Euphorbia
Succulent in the Euphorbia Family

Height: To 30'	**Blooms:** Winter
Exposure: Sun, partial shade	**Hardiness:** 50°F.

Because of their strong, uniquely defined shapes, euphorbias make excellent house plants by serving the

Euphorbia canariensis

Euphorbia bupleurifolia

Euphorbia aggregata

Euphorbia...

each species unique, boldly shaped

Euphorbia milii (crown of thorns)

Foreground: *E. meleformis, E. obesa*
Background: *E. horrida, E. lactea cristata* (crested euphorbia)

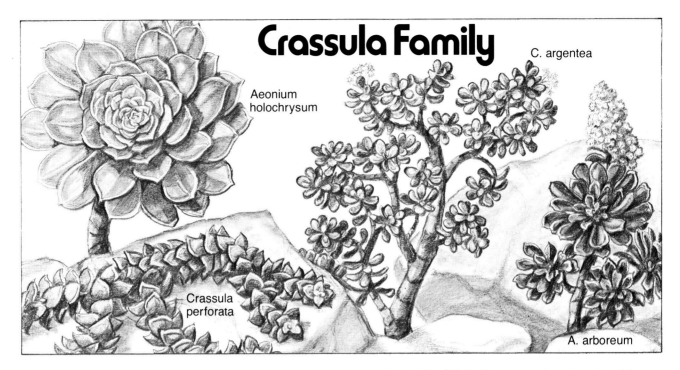

Crassula Family

Aeonium holochrysum

C. argentea

Crassula perforata

A. arboreum

From a tiny, half-inch cluster of *Sempervivum arachnoideum* to woody, almost tree-size shrubs like *Crassula argentea* and *Aeonium arboreum*, the Crassula family represents an outstanding variety of succulents for home and garden settings. Included are *Aeonium, Crassula, Echeveria, Sedum, Cotyledon, Kalanchoe, Sempervivum*, and *Dudleya*.

Aeonium
Succulent in the Crassula Family

Height: To 4'

Exposure: Sun, partial shade

Blooms: Winter, spring, summer

Hardiness: 30°F.

Decorative aeoniums are rosette-forming plants. They form a clustering base in the bushier species, or sit high atop sturdy stems in others. Brightly colored flowers—yellow, red, white, or pink—appear in spring, though a few varieties choose to bloom in the dead of winter or early summer. Unfortunately, flower-bearing parts will wither and die; some plants, though, are able to sprout new shoots and begin again.

Aeonium arboreum. Golden yellow, 8-inch flowers top erect stems. Rosettes are flattened, bright green. Most common variety, *A. a.*'Atropurpureum,' characterized by purplish leaves; 'Zwartkop' has black leaves.

A. canariense (VELVET ROSE, CANARY ISLAND AEONIUM). Enormous rosettes reach 2 feet wide, covered with smooth white hairs. Yellow flowers.

A. floribunda. Unusual species. Lemon yellow blooms in summer. (Photo on facing page.)

A. haworthii (PINWHEEL). Widely grown. Leaves are blue green, often tinged with red at edges. Shrubby growth to 2 feet high. Creamy-colored, spring blooms.

A. undulatum (SAUCER PLANT, DINNER PLATE). Dark, glossy leaves on single stems; yellow blooms.

Crassula
Succulent in the Crassula Family

Height: To 10'

Exposure: Sun

Blooms: Spring, summer

Hardiness: 45°F.

Container gardeners take note: practically all crassulas adore the confines of container living. They can thrive in the same pot for years, requiring little more than the basics—a good bright location and ample food and water during the growing season.

Crassula arborescens (SILVER DOLLAR). Thick, fleshy, grayish leaves are edged with red. White or pink flowers appear only on mature plants.

C. argentea (JADE PLANT, JADE TREE). Fast-growing species characterized by thick, woody stems and fleshy, gray green leaves. Ideal potted plant.

C. falcata (AIRPLANE PLANT). Shrubby growth to 3 feet. Bright scarlet flowers; thick gray green leaves.

C. lycopodioides (WATCH CHAIN, TOY CYPRESS). Easily grown both indoors and out. Tiny, yellowish green flowers.

C. perforata (STRING OF BUTTONS). Opposite pairs of flattened, pale green leaves are joined at ends. Minute yellow flowers appear in early spring.

C. rupestris (BUTTONS-ON-A-STRING). Thick, overlapping leaves grow in spreading habit. Good potted subject.

Crassula Family...

Aeonium floribunda

Aeonium urbicum (foreground), *Aeonium arboreum* 'Atropurpureum'

creepers and trailers,
hardy shrubs, or
crowned with rosettes

Sedum nussbaumeranum

Crassula species

More Crassula Family...

leaves cluster in groups or overlap

Sedum rubrotinctum (pork and beans)

Clockwise, from top: *Sedum morganianum* (donkey tail), *Sedum globosum*, *Sedum rubrotinctum*

or have colorful rosettes and delicate flowers

Echeveria agavoides (molded wax)

Yellow-flowering echeveria

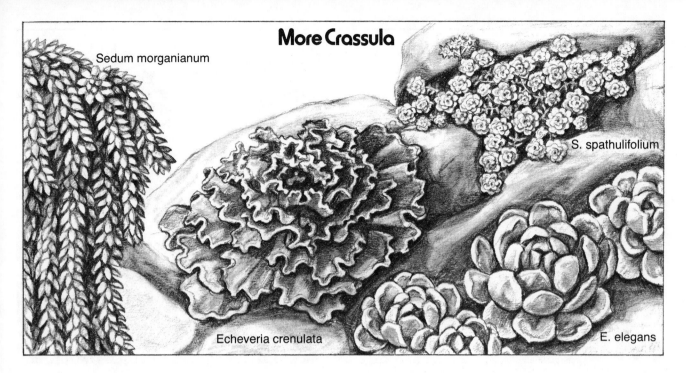

More Crassula

Sedum morganianum

S. spathulifolium

Echeveria crenulata

E. elegans

Sedum
Succulent in the Crassula Family

Height: To 3′   **Blooms:** Throughout year

Exposure: Sun   **Hardiness:** 35°F. or lower

Sedums have a lot going for them: unusual coloring, fast growth, and hardiness—even in poor, unimproved soil. They are small succulents, usually under 8 inches high, but despite their size, sedums offer gardeners many growing opportunities. Some are excellent potted plants for window or dish gardens or hanging baskets. Hardier ones make colorful ground covers or dependable plants for rock gardens or retaining walls.

Sedum acre (WALL PEPPER, GOLD MOSS). Creeping growth of tiny, overlapping leaves; yellow blooms.

S. dasyphyllum. Carpet of blue green leaves and white flowers with pink edges. Used in rock gardens.

S. morganianum (DONKEY'S TAIL). Ever-popular hanging basket succulent. Small, fleshy stems hang over pot's edge, red flowers. (Photo on facing page.)

S. pachyphyllum (JELLY BEANS, MANY FINGERS). Low shrubby growth with cylindrical, blue green leaves; yellow flowers.

S. rubrotinctum (PORK AND BEANS). Wintertime yellow flowers cover this 8-inch-high sedum whose leaves are bright green tinged with yellow and red. Excellent for dish gardens; hardy to 20°. (Photo on facing page.)

S. sieboldii. Graceful, hanging sedum has scallop-edged, bluish leaves; clusters of pink flowers. To −20°.

S. spathulifolium. Inch-tall sedum, growing in tiny, fleshy rosettes, bears small, starry yellow flowers. To −10°; evergreen in warm-winter areas.

S. spectabile. Easy-to-grow, late summer bloomer. Tiny pink flowers grow in flat, fluffy clusters; to −25°. Completely dormant in winter.

Echeveria
Succulent in the Crassula Family

Height: To 3′   **Blooms:** Throughout year

Exposure: Sun, partial shade   **Hardiness:** 30°F.

Handsome, fleshy-leafed echeveria rosettes look geometrically perfect in some species and are said to resemble flowers rather than plants. Because much hybridizing has occurred, many echeverias have reached spectacularly large proportions and are thus highly prized for their shape, color, and leaf texture. The genus is commonly called hen and chicks, and descriptions are listed for over 100 known species.

Echeveria agavoides (MOLDED WAX). Pointed tips of light green rosette are tinged with red. Red and yellow flowers (Photo on facing page.)

E. derenbergii (PAINTED LADY). Pale green rosette looks like miniature artichoke. Reddish yellow flowers in winter, spring.

E. elegans (PEARL ECHEVERIA). Densely leafed rosette is somewhat translucent; produces offsets readily. Reddish yellow blooms.

E. pulvinata (CHENILLE PLANT). Flattened leaves covered with fine, white hairs; red and yellow flowers.

E. setosa (MEXICAN FIRECRACKER). Dark green, 4-inch-wide rosette has white hairs, red blooms.

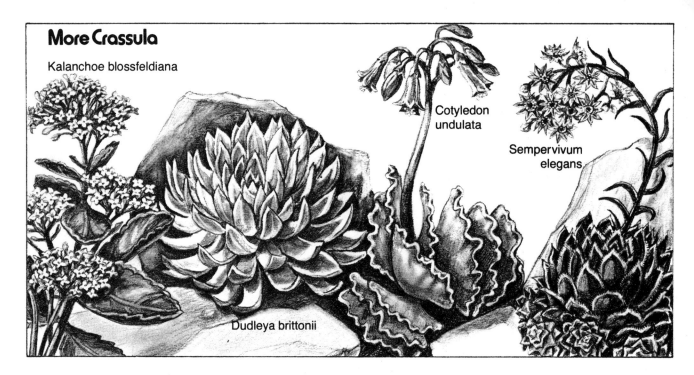

More Crassula

Kalanchoe blossfeldiana

Cotyledon undulata

Sempervivum elegans

Dudleya brittonii

Cotyledon
Succulent in the Crassula Family

Height: To 4′ **Blooms:** Summer
Exposure: Sun **Hardiness:** 45°F.

Cotyledons, prized for their outstanding bold forms and interesting leaves, make up the next genus in the Crassula family.

Cotyledon orbiculata. Waxy gray leaves, often margined in red. Two-foot stalks bear bell-shaped, reddish yellow blooms.

C. undulata (SILVER CROWN). Popular species characterized by wavy, fluted leaves and yellow orange flowers. Care should be taken not to water from above.

Kalanchoe
Succulent in the Crassula Family

Height: To 8′ **Blooms:** Winter
Exposure: Sun, **Hardiness:** 45°F.
partial shade

Kalanchoes are tropical natives, thus preferring a moist, environment with little threat of frost.

Kalanchoe beharensis (VELVET ELEPHANT EAR). Treelike, silvery felted plant has crimped furry leaves; up to 8 feet. Good indoor or outdoor plant.

K. blossfeldiana. Popular Christmas plant. Green waxy leaves with red, yellow, orange, or salmon flowers.

K. tomentosa (PANDA PLANT). Tapered, white-felted leaves covered with brown dots. Very attractive potted plant.

Dudleya
Succulent in the Crassula Family

Height: To 2′ **Blooms:** Spring,
summer
Exposure: Partial **Hardiness:** 20°–35°F.
shade

Striking in appearance, dudleyas are rosette-forming succulents with fleshy leaves that are covered with a heavy coat of chalky powder.

Dudleya brittonii. Powdery white, brittle leaves form a single rosette. Large species reach 2 feet wide.

D. farinosa. Widely cultivated. Small clustering habit with pale yellow, summer blooms. California native.

Sempervivum
Succulent in the Crassula Family

Height: To 6″ **Blooms:** Summer
Exposure: Partial **Hardiness:** 25°F.
shade or lower

Popularly called houseleeks, sempervivums are small, rosette-forming plants, some less than ½-inch wide. Growing in clusters; popular in rock gardens.

Sempervivum arachnoideum (COBWEB HOUSE-LEEK). Gray green, hairy leaves laced together with silver webs.

S. elegans. Also sold as *S. barbulatum*. Used most often in hybridizing; tiny rosettes and flowers.

S. tectorum (HEN AND CHICKS). Bristle-pointed leaves are tipped with reddish brown.

Milkweed

Ceropegia woodii

Stapelia

Huernia confusa

Stapelia gigantea (ZULU GIANT, GIANT STARFISH). Enormous flowers, some reaching 18 inches wide, are creamy yellow with red edges.

S. variegata (TOAD CACTUS). Fingerlike stems are fleshy, stubby; yellow flowers spotted with purple.

Ceropegia
Succulent in the Milkweed Family

Height: To 10′ **Blooms:** Summer
Exposure: Sun, **Hardiness:** 35°F.
partial shade

Ceropegias are either quick-growing, shrubby plants or vining ones with tuberous roots. Not only are they dependable house plants because they withstand dry, warm conditions, but they also make an excellent choice for hanging baskets outdoors.

Ceropegia barkleyi. Oval green leaves, veined with white, grow on trailing stems. Slender, funnel-shaped flowers are white with light purple markings.

C. woodii (ROSARY VINE, STRING OF HEARTS). Heart-shaped leaves, marbled with silver, grow on trailing stems. Tiny purple blooms.

Huernia
Succulent in the Milkweed Family

Height: To 14″ **Blooms:** Summer,
autumn
Exposure: Sun, **Hardiness:** 35°F.
partial shade

Huernia—a dwarf succulent whose angled stems are toothed or notched—is another genus in the Milkweed family. This intricate little plant, sometimes no more than 4 inches high, grows slowly in clusters.

Huernia confusa (LIFESAVER PLANT). Tiny, unique species remains under 4 inches high; glossy, yellow and maroon flower is star-shaped. (See page 50.)

H. zebrina (ZEBRA FLOWER, OWL'S EYES). Short, 5-angled stems bear yellow flowers tinged with red.

Other milkweeds

Though it is impossible to include many of the 2,000 species of succulents considered part of the Milkweed family, here are a few widely cultivated species:

Caralluma burchardii. Four-angled, almost square-stemmed species bears clusters of dainty yellow and brown flowers.

Hoodia bainii. Cup-shaped, nearly round flowers are light yellow, edged with pink. Curiously rare succulent.

Hoya carnosa (WAX PLANT). Trailing, fleshy ovate leaves are bright green; whorls of waxy, pinkish flowers appear in summer. Excellent, dependable house plant.

The milkweed family includes *Stapelia*, *Ceropegia*, *Huernia*, and others; they are juicy-stemmed succulents, either vining or growing upright, that bear beautifully intricate flowers.

Stapelia
Succulent in the Milkweed Family

Height: To 12″ **Blooms:** Summer,
autumn
Exposure: Sun, **Hardiness:** 35°F.
partial shade

The genus *Stapelia* has two nicknames: starfish flower, appropriately chosen because of its five-pointed appearance, and carrion flower. Unfortunately, the latter accurately describes the foul-smelling odor given off by the bloom. It shouldn't bother you any more than the fact that stapelias depend on flies for pollination. Just remember—beautifully flowering stapelias are unique in appearance and worthy of cultivation.

Lily

Aloe arborescens

Gasteria verrucosa

A. variegata

Haworthia retusa

Though taxonomists list nearly 250 different genera in the Lily family *(Liliaceae),* **most of the leafy succulents are found in** *Aloe, Gasteria,* **and** *Haworthia.*

Aloe
Succulent in the Lily Family

Height: To 60′ **Blooms:** Throughout year

Exposure: Sun, partial shade **Hardiness:** 20°–35°F.

Take your pick—there's an aloe that blooms every month of the year, though the biggest show is from February to September. Ranging from 6-inch miniatures to 60-foot trees, their appearance is strikingly similar: clumps of fleshy, pointed leaves, usually green or gray green with contrasting bands or streaks. Flowers grow in clusters in orange, red, and yellow.

Aloe arborescens (TREE ALOE, CANDELABRA ALOE). Hardy (to 30°F.) species withstands drought,

sun, salt spray, and shade. Branching stems carry big clumps of spiny-edged leaves. Wintertime flowers are bright vermilion to clear yellow.

A. barbadensis (UNGUENTINE CACTUS, MEDICINAL ALOE). Easy-to-grow, attractive aloe has analgesic pulp that soothes minor burns. Good potted plant for kitchen window.

A. mitriformis (PURPLE CROWN). Horny teeth edge fleshy leaves. (Photo on facing page.)

A. nobilis. Dark green leaves edged with small, hooked teeth; 2-foot stalks bear red orange blooms.

A. saponaria. Short-stemmed, broad, clumping plant with variegated leaves, long-lasting reddish orange flowers. (Photo on facing page.)

A. variegata (PARTRIDGE BREAST, TIGER ALOE). Dark green, 5-inch leaves are banded and edged with white. Loose flower clusters, red or pink, bloom throughout year.

Gasteria
Succulent in the Lily Family

Height: 1′ **Blooms:** Spring

Exposure: All exposures **Hardiness:** 35°F.

Nicknamed lawyer's tongue or cow tongue cactus, gasterias are similar to aloes except that their leaves are two-ranked (oppositely produced), thus presenting a random rather than symmetrical appearance.

Gasteria maculata. Thick, tongue-shaped, fleshy leaves are mottled with white and twist in spiral growth. Red flowers appear in clusters on tall stalks.

G. verrucosa (WARTY ALOE). Sharply tapered leaves are covered with prominent white warts (tubercles).

Haworthia
Succulent in the Lily Family

Height: To 1′ **Blooms:** Summer

Exposure: Partial shade **Hardiness:** 35°F.

Haworthias are one of the best choices for potted indoor plants because of their compact size, tolerance for shade, and fascinating leaf formations.

Haworthia attenuata. Dull pink flowers; leaves marked with white warts.

H. fasciata (FAIRY WASHBOARD). Zebra-striped rosette and greenish white blooms. (Photo on facing page.)

H. retusa. Checkered lines on glossy green leaves. Fine white teeth edge the sides of rosette.

H. setata (LACE HAWORTHIA). Small stemless rosettes of many leaves; bristly white teeth give it a lacy look.

Haworthia fasciata (fairy washboard)

Flower of Aloe saponaria

Lilies...

pointed, fleshy leaves
and showy flowers

Aloe mitriformis

Yellow-flowering agave

Agave americana

Agave...

bold, sword-shaped leaves,
occasional bloom

Agave parviflora

Sansevieria 'Hahnii'

Agave and Daisy

Agave americana 'Marginata'

Senecio stapeliiformis

Sansevieria trifasciata 'Laurentii'

"Hard working" describes the Agave family *(Agavaceae)*. Plants are grown as ornamentals, used by fiber-producing industries, and in fermentation processes by distillers.

Agave
Succulent in the Agave Family

Height: To 15′ **Blooms:** Once
Exposure: Sun **Hardiness:** 25°F. or lower

Known for their hardiness and tolerance to adverse conditions, agaves have long been used in desert landscapes, especially where bold forms are needed.

Agave americana (CENTURY PLANT, MAGUEY). Hooked spines edge 6-foot-long, blue green leaves. After 10 years or more, plant produces stalk with yellowish green flowers almost 40 feet in the air. *A. a. marginata* has yellow-edged leaves.

A. attenuata. Big, bold, but spineless leaves are sword-shaped and grow in wide rosettes.

A. parviflora. Olive green leaves, trimmed with white, form colorful rosette. (Photo on facing page.)

A. victoriae-reginae. Spectacularly marked olive green leaves have pencil-thin white edges. Slow-growing, it will stand in pot or ground 20 years.

Sansevieria
Succulent in the Agave Family

Height: To 5′ **Blooms:** Seldom
Exposure: All exposures **Hardiness:** 35°F.

Popularly grown as house plants for generations, these dependable succulents endure dry air, little light, uneven temperatures, and infrequent waterings.

S. trifasciata (SNAKE PLANT, MOTHER-IN-LAW'S TONGUE). Stiffly erect, 4-foot leaves are dark green, broadly banded with silvery gray. Variety 'Laurentii' is popular as is 'Hahnii' (BIRD'S NEST SANSEVIERIA), whose short leaves form a funnel-shaped rosette. (Photo on facing page.)

Yuccas

Often grouped with agaves, these evergreen perennials are desert tree plants. They do best in full sun; most take considerable drought when established but will accept garden watering. Hardiness to 30°F. or lower.

Yucca aloifolia (SPANISH BAYONET). Pointed, sharp green leaves; single trunk or branched to 10 feet.

Y. brevifolia (JOSHUA TREE). Slow-growing with thick trunk and short, broad, sword-shaped leaves.

Y. elephantipes (GIANT YUCCA). Fast-growing to 25–30 feet. Creamy white flowers in spring.

Y. glauca (SMALL SOAPWEED). Summer flowers are pale white; leaves are edged with white and 2 feet long.

Y. whipplei (OUR LORD'S CANDLE). Dense cluster of 2-foot-long, pointed leaves. Hardy to −15°F.; spectacular blooms.

The Daisy Family

Though the Daisy family *(Compositae)* is one of the largest of the entire plant world, its succulent members number just one—*Senecio*. Formerly separated into other genera such as *Kleinia* and *Othonna*, these succulents are now grouped together by most taxonomists.

Senecio articulatus (CANDLE PLANT, HOT DOG CACTUS). Swollen, segmented stems are bluish gray. Easy-to-grow, attractive.

S. stapeliiformis (CANDY STICK). Unusual species. Erect, many-angled stems grow horizontally below ground before emerging. Summertime flowers are scarlet.

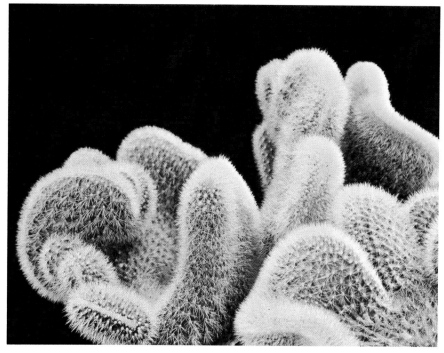

Weberbauerocereus winterianus. See page 14.

Opuntia ramosissima (pencil cholla).
See page 11.

Hildawinteria aureispina. See page 28.

... too curious for words

Huernia confusa (lifesaver plant). See page 45.

Mesembryanthemum

Lampranthus

Conophytum

Lithops

We saved the most curious succulent family for last. Within the Mesembryanthemum family are thousands of species, almost all of which are native to South Africa. Like other succulents, they adapted, withstanding the worst conditions nature offered. In order to survive, one inventive group, commonly called flowering stones, mimicked nature by simulating the appearance of surrounding rocks and pebbles. Only when they bloomed could they be recognized as plants. Growing low on the ground, their somewhat rounded shape enabled them to conserve the greatest amount of moisture.

Flowering stones

Flowering stones grow best in a fine soil mix of equal parts sand and soil. Be sure containers have ample drainage because these plants will not tolerate stagnant soil. During cold or cloudy weather (and throughout winter), do not give them any water. Only when growth begins should water be applied, and then only moderately. Flowering stones like fresh air, some sun, and temperatures above 50°F.

There are over 20 genera that have flowering stone plants. Some of them include:

Lithops (STONEFACE). Shaped like an inverted, flattened cone, lithops look like smooth stones with a fissure across the middle. From this fissure emerge new leaves and the large, daisylike flower. Preferring a well-lighted location, lithops make fascinating indoor plants, especially when blooming from July to November. Flowers, usually yellow or white, appear in the afternoon, then close at night. *Lithops dinteri*, *L. karasmontana*, and *L. pseudotruncatella* are some better-known species.

Conophytum. Conophytums resemble the *Lithops* species but the leaves are joined with only a slight cleft

at the top. They are rounded, cone shaped, flat-sided plants ranging in size from ½ inch to 4 inches high. Most are gray with veins or marbling on the foliage. Nicknamed cone plants, they bear autumn flowers more colorful than most—yellow, pink, red, purple, and white. *Conophytum giftbergensis*, *C. minutum*, and *C. pearsonii* are attractive sorts worthy trying.

Pleiospilos (STONE MIMICRY PLANT). Clustering in groups, tiny pleiospilos have a unique appearance: their form and coloring are true miracles in mimicry. Angular brownish gray or brownish green pairs of leaves are covered with dark raised spots, suggesting a pile of weathered granite pebbles rather than plants. Yellow flowers, up to 3 inches across, appear in autumn. *Pleiospilos bolusi* (AFRICAN LIVING ROCK), *P. magnipunctatus*, *P. nelii* (SPLIT ROCK), and *P. simularis* are all popular.

Other mesembryanthemums

Faucaria (TIGER JAWS). Very fleshy, triangular leaves, growing into angular rosettes, have toothed edges. Leaves are grayish green, sometimes tinged with red and spotted. Large, yellow or white daisylike blooms appear from August to November. *F. bosscheana* and *F. tigrina* (TIGER'S JAW) are popular species.

Many dwarf, shrubby mesembryanthemum species were once conveniently lumped together. Now they are classified under several different genera—*Carpobrotus*, *Cephalophyllum*, *Delosperma*, *Drosanthemum*, *Lampranthum*, and *Maleophora*. Known commonly as ice plants, these species are quick-growing, free-flowering plants that have long been valued as indestructible ground covers in mild winter areas or as potted plants elsewhere.

For an extensive list of ice plants that includes blooming periods and ways to grow them, see page 61.

Where Will They Grow?

"Where *Won't* They Grow?" might have been a better title for this chapter, because despite the fallacy that they grow only in deserts, succulent plants can be raised almost everywhere. Inside your home or out in the garden, under a tree, down a steep hillside, along a fence, or even in between rocks—there are so many possibilities for raising cacti and succulents, adequate space may be your only limitation.

Grown in attractive pots, dish gardens, and terrariums, succulents can be displayed as house plants, in window gardens, or in hanging baskets. Or raise them in less formal containers—clay or plastic pots—in lath houses, greenhouses, or other simple display structures.

Outdoors, integrate succulents into landscapes as ground covers or edgings, in rock gardens, or as companions to other ornamentals; more casual varieties can be planted in small sections of a border or in corners of the garden. And if you're really ambitious and have a special collection to show off, why not plant them in rows or plots, staked off and labeled—just like an arboretum?

More than an ordinary house plant

Lush, leafy house plants move in and out of many homes with predictable regularity. Attempts to grow some popular varieties often fail when conditions are so poor that plants can't adapt. Dry, hot rooms with little ventilation or simple neglect mark the fatal end of many house plants.

Recently, there has been a discovery (actually, a rediscovery) that succulents make excellent house plants. They adapt naturally to dry, warm temperatures and withstand poor care for days, even weeks at a time. But beyond their dependability—some call it indestructibility—lies the fact that they're also quite beautiful.

In what other group of plants do you find such an assortment? Specimen-size succulent plants, raised where they can be viewed at close range, seldom fail to arouse interest. Their sculptural habit and the variety of leaf sizes, shapes, and arrangements are—in many species—combined with striking color patterns that contribute to their fascination.

Display upright and tree-type succulents in large containers where their textures and colors can be enhanced by different kinds of flooring. These same plants can be dramatically silhouetted against a light-colored wall, or softly illuminated with well-placed spotlights. Groups of rosette-forming succulents such as echeverias and sempervivums show off their delicately scalloped leaves best when displayed in shallow containers on low tabletops so that their patterns or growth habit can be viewed from above.

It is important to give indoor succulent plants as much light as possible. If there is little natural light, put them near lamps or under overhead light fixtures. A periodic turn helps keep plants in shady locations from becoming one-sided.

Besides sensing their intrinsic value, many people consider potted cacti and succulents decorative elements that can be used in a number of imaginative ways. Display them in bookcases, on tabletops, and windowsills; use them singly or in groups in entryways and halls; or suspend some hanging types from the ceiling. Just about any well-lighted spot lends itself to succulent plants. The only thing to remember when displaying a favorite cactus—indoors or outdoors—is to leave ample room to get around it.

Since nurseries usually grow cacti and succulents in clay or plastic pots, you may want to hide the pots in more decorative containers.

Window gardens

A window-lined garden room is the perfect location for a large cactus or succulent: it provides good, even light throughout the day without the damaging effect caused by harsh, direct sunlight. If you don't have such a room, but still enjoy plants indoors, find a well-exposed windowsill instead.

Small and medium-size plants are best suited for a window scene, while larger types require more space—possibly outdoors. Good window subjects include haworthias, small agaves and aloes, and many young or compact cacti like rebutias and mammillarias.

A conglomeration of large plants in a small window area tends to create an untidy picture, so you may want to limit your selections.

Careful selection can help in another way. Because succulent plants don't all bloom at the same time of the year—most cacti flower in summer—you can have color for several months by knowing and choosing plants according to when they bloom.

All window exposures can be used—even a north-facing windowsill is all right for some crassulas and sedums—but east and south-facing sills provide the best location for growing healthy plants. Occasionally in summer, plants too close to the window glass may burn. A screen or a light curtain will provide adequate shade if you don't wish to move plants away from the window altogether.

Average home temperatures—about 65°F. during the day and 10–15° cooler at night—are fine for most succulents. As long as indoor temperatures remain above 45°F., most plants exist comfortably. On severe nights, though, some newspaper taped up against the glass will offer added protection from the cold.

Unlike other house plants, cacti and succulents are not too fussy about humidity (moisture in the air). Most homes have between 10 and 20 percent humidity in the air, and this is sufficient for succulent plants. They do need clean, well-circulated air, though; a stuffy, hot atmosphere can harm any plant. A well-ventilated room should be provided: keep a window slightly open but not so far open that plants are exposed to a draft.

A vital part of successful succulent growing is the yearly rest (see page 77). Once a year—almost always in winter—plants begin to enter their dormant period. Designate some out-of-the-way spot where there is some light but cooler temperatures (about 50°F.) as a rest area: a pantry, an unheated but not freezing porch, or a lighted basement are good choices. As plants stop growing, relocate them to the rest area and decrease watering. During the rest period give them just enough water to keep soil barely moist and plants from shriveling. Most species like dry periods between applications. When growth resumes—some time in spring—return plants to their places at the window and begin regular watering again.

Listed here are some cacti and succulents for window gardens or indoor use, representing a wide variety of growth forms and foliage colors.

Aeoniums: *A. arboreum 'Atropurpureum', A. canariense*
Agaves: *A. filifera, A. picta, A. stricta, A. victoriae-reginae*
Aloes: *A. nobilis, A. striata, A. variegata*
Astrophytums: *A. capricorne, A. ornatum*
Cephalocereus: *C. palmeri, C. senilis*
Crassulas: *C. arborescens, C. argentea, C. lycopodioidea*
Echeverias: *E. derenbergii, E. elegans, E. pulvinata*
Echinocactus: *E. grusonii*
Echinocereus: *E. ehrenbergii, E. pectinatus, E. reichenbachii*
Euphorbias: *E. lactea, E. milii, E. obesa*
Kalanchoes: *K. blossfeldiana, K. tomentosa*
Mammillarias: *M. bocasana, M. fragilis, M. spinosissima.*
Notocactus: *N. haselbergii, N. ottonis, N. schumannianus, N. scopa*
Opuntias: *O. basilaris, O. microdasys,*
Parodias: *P. aureispina, P. sanguiniflora*
Rebutias: *R. kupperana, R. minuscula*
Sedums: *S. multiceps, S. spectabile*

In dish gardens

The desert fascinates most people enough so that many have bought or planted their own dish garden of cacti or succulent plants. These miniature desert scenes (some may look tropical, depending on the succulent plants) are scale-model replicas of larger panoramas. Displayed in attractive containers, most dish gardens are planted with slow-growing species that remain small, attractive subjects for years.

You can buy tiny gardens already planted from nurseries or florists, or you may want to make your own. It takes only a few hours, and once the plants are established, the dish garden will grow almost unattended.

Your first step is to select an appropriate dish. Desert plants can be grown in terrariums, glass bowls, aquariums, brandy snifters, or just about any other container that holds soil. It can be any shape—round, square, rectangle—but it must be deep enough to hold at least 2 inches of soil. For indoor desert gardens, a simple container is best; choose one that has a color and texture that is complementary to the plants it will contain. Outdoor dish gardens can be planted in larger ceramic or decorative clay pots, or even in hanging wire-framed baskets (see opposite page). Just make sure your container provides sufficient drainage so there is no danger of overwatering. If no drainage hole exists, 2 inches of gravel on the bottom of the container helps guard against soggy soil.

Carefully remove plants from their original containers, making sure root ball is intact. Set them in your dish and shift them around until you decide exactly where you want them. Your design work will be easier if you start with a dominant plant—an interestingly formed cactus for example—and work other plants around it. Use the textures, forms, and colors of plants to create a living picture. Add soil to within ½ inch of the rim of the dish and set plants in place. Do not water the dish immediately—wait a few days; then give scanty moisture for a few weeks.

How much and how often to water is the secret to keeping dish gardens handsome. Dry-looking surface soil may be soggy underneath, so dig down carefully with a plastic plant label or your finger to be sure water is really needed. If soil adheres to the plastic label when removed, you still have enough moisture in the dish. Always apply water with great care; moisten the soil gently, never flood it. Locate in a bright sunny spot either indoors or out.

Dish Gardens

Scale-model species create miniature desert scene; all are slow growers that thrive in confines of shallow dish garden.

Crassulas, echeverias, sedum combine with natural stone, pieces of driftwood for attractive outdoor dish garden. Design: Lew Whitney.

Eye-level attraction created by moss-lined wire basket of hanging succulents includes *Aeonium decorum*, Irish moss, begonias, echeverias. Design: Lew Whitney.

Indoor Ideas

Smooth, waxy skin of *Opuntia quimilo* sharply contrasts with 6-inch-long, white spines. Find a spot far out of reach of children, pets, heavy traffic.

Tabletop assortment of small cacti looks attractive in handmade ceramic pots; locate near well-lighted window.

Bright, sunny windowsill hosts compact cacti; wrought iron mesh screen helps prevent burning from harsh sunlight. From left: *Echinopsis hammerschmidtii, Trichocereus spachianus* (golden torch), and *Tephrocactus boliviensis.*

Delicate **Crassula socialis** puts on spectacular, midwinter show with clusters of tiny, pure white blooms.

Bold, dramatic forms of *Ferocactus acanthodes* (foreground) and *Cereus peruvianus* silhouette against corner windows. Large species with such fascinating, intricate spination become focal points of room—especially when viewed close up.

Lath Houses and Greenhouses

Greenhouse collection of cacti, raised in single planter box, are grouped, labeled according to genera. Area below planters offers storage space for additional equipment, soil mixes.

Tiered wooden benches, mounted on support beams inside lath house, hold dozens of potted cacti.

Typical cactus greenhouse has "bulging-at-the-seams" look. Removable window supplies good ventilation; sloping roof provides extra room for tall, columnar torches.

Plants thrive in lath houses...

In mild climate areas, many hobbyists house their cacti and succulent collections in simple, greenhouse-type structures built of wood lath strips. Popularly called lath houses, these structures offer many of the same advantages as greenhouses without the added cost of insulation and heating. The open-air sides and roof provide good, natural light as well as excellent ventilation.

Controlling the temperature in a lath house is the real disadvantage. Some protection from cold night temperatures can be provided with heavy shades—canvas, plastic, or other similar materials—that are lowered down over the sides at the end of the day. But in areas where night temperatures fall below 40–45°F., it would be wiser to keep succulent plants in an insulated greenhouse instead.

The lath house pictured on the opposite page is equipped with tiered shelves that display cacti and succulents of various heights, with shades that pull down to protect tender plants from extremely hot, burning sun. Measuring 6 by 8 feet, a lath house like this can easily accommodate 150 to 200 potted plants.

...and in greenhouses

Good lighting and ventilation, sufficient heat, and protection from damaging frost and hot sun—these are the reasons cacti and succulents thrive in greenhouses.

Greenhouses offer the best, most easily controlled environment for most plants, whether you live in warm desert areas and use your greenhouse as protection from the sun, or in colder areas where a greenhouse is the only way plants survive through winter.

Most structures have clear or white roofs, usually of rigid plastic, that produce the optimum amount of brightness without harmful, burning sunlight. Various shapes are available including: lean-to and conventional even-span varieties, quonset-shaped ones, geodesic domes, and A-frames. Many are prefabricated, combining wood with glass or plastic, and people who are at all handy usually have little or no difficulty assembling the units.

A must for cactus and succulent care is good ventilation. Circulating fans and automatic vents can provide this, as well as ventilating strips and other openings through which hot air can escape. Lightweight wall panels, taken off during weather extremes, can also increase fresh air circulation. Some types are mounted on hinges that swing panels upward; others hang from hooks and are removed altogether.

Concrete, bricks, stones, wooden slats, gravel, ground bark, and sawdust are all possible coverings for greenhouse floors. Depending on the kind of greenhouse you have, where you live, and how much you want to spend, these choices are varied enough to suit everyone's needs.

Benches, placed around the inside perimeter of the greenhouse, are used to hold plants, propagating trays, seed flats, and other supplies. Some are flat,

while others are tiered like stairs—each step wide enough to hold a single row of succulents. The most efficient way to save space is with tiered benches since you get many more plants on the vertical shelves than you would on a flat bench that uses the same amount of floor space. Larger, tall columnar cacti can be set on the lowest tier and still have room above without touching the greenhouse roof.

Since cacti and succulents like to dry out somewhat between waterings, many hobbyists grow their greenhouse plants in clay pots. (Clay is porous, allowing dry air in and moisture out.) Plastic pots can be used too, but be careful to avoid overwatering—a rotten, usually inevitable end for most succulent plants.

Some more enthusiastic collectors plant their specimens directly into beds of soil. The greenhouse pictured at right on the opposite page is fitted with raised planter boxes. The owner has carefully selected her cacti, planting and arranging them so that different genera are grouped together.

Greenhouses offer a practical way to care for large numbers of succulent plants. Ventilation, light, and temperature can be controlled, offering each plant the incentive to bloom and the opportunity for optimum health.

...or planted outdoors

As beautiful as they are indoors or in a greenhouse, cacti and succulents truly come into their own when they move outside. Foliage colors become more intense, growth appears more vigorous, and many plants produce a more prolific bloom. Their interesting shapes and varied forms make these plants outstanding candidates for achieving dramatic outdoor pictures—especially if you garden in the West or Southwest. But even where summers are short—in the Midwest, for example—potted plants sunk in the ground or displayed on a patio can add distinction and beauty to your garden. During severely cold months these plants can be relocated in a greenhouse or on a protected porch until spring comes the following year.

Large types of succulent plants are often used like sculpture, silhouetted against house or sky. A tall, columnar cereus or palmlike yucca, as well as some of the larger sword-leafed agaves, give a bold and assertive appearance. Mounding mammillarias, echinocereus, and some crassulas are effective where medium height and spreading masses are needed. Low-growing aeoniums, echeverias, and ice plants create handsomely patterned, living carpets of color for hillsides, under trees, even in between rocks. In summer, when the brilliant flowers of ground cover types appear, be ready for a spectacular display.

Cactus for outdoor plantings can be divided into three types based on growth forms: the cereus type and its allies with thick, branched or treelike growth; globular or low-growing kinds including ball and melon shapes; and echinocacti—plants with a single, usually unbranched body in barrel or cylindrical shapes.

Succulents can be grouped into four types: the rosette-forming varieties, the sword-shaped aloes and agaves, small shrubby types (cotyledons, crassulas), and the crawling ground covers.

You can see how versatile succulent plants are. They offer a tremendous variety of shapes, forms, textures, leaf colors, and flowers, but still retain the most important advantage of all—low maintenance.

A great choice for containers

Patios, porches, terraces, decks, and balconies all share something in common. Unlike other outdoor areas where soil is readily available, these locations depend on containers if plants are to be grown at all.

In most outdoor living spaces, potted cacti and succulents make handsome accents, and because many are practically maintenance-free, they become even more attractive. Grown in pots or boxes, barrels or tubs, they can be placed so as to relieve the monotony along the side of a house, or to enliven an entryway, driveway, or expanse of stucco wall.

Ball and melon-type cacti make especially interesting container subjects; they are highly desirable when something "different" is needed. A large, sword-shaped aloe or agave, displayed in a decorative container, can be the focal point of interest in a previously unimaginative area.

Since patio plants are always on display, pick the most unusual, attractive ones for the greatest interest and enjoyment. Round, beautifully spined species like *Echinocactus grusonii* (golden barrel) and *Notocactus leninghausii* (golden ball cactus) are just right for pots or tubs with similarly rounded edges. Tapered, Spanish pots are good for displaying plants with more haphazard growth—*Opuntia microdasys* (bunny ears) and *O. bigelovii* (teddy bear cactus) are good choices. A large, distinctive container takes on new importance when planted with a bold, columnar cereus.

Dependable as ground covers

Decorative, low-maintenance ground covers are proving to be a popular alternative to lawns in many areas these days. Perhaps it is because most grow well in spots where other plants fail—down hillsides, under trees, or around rocks. They spread rapidly in most cases, succeed in the poorest soils, and provide brilliant color in spring and summer. Many kinds of succulents also find conditions to their liking on wall gardens or retaining walls and thrive for years almost unattended. In mild-winter areas or along the coasts, some ground covers have replaced lawns altogether.

Good candidates for no-traffic ground covers are found in many succulent genera. Senecios, with their fleshy stems and thistlelike flowers, are popular; perhaps the most commonly used species is *Senecio repens* with its blue green, cylindrical leaves and tiny white flowers. Similar but larger are *S. ficoides* and *S. mandraliscae*—both from 12–18 inches tall.

Sedums, too, make fine ground covers in small areas where unusual texture and color are needed. Soft and easily crushed, they will not take foot traffic; otherwise,

they are tough, low-maintenance ground covers. Because there is a great difference in hardiness among sedums—some species tolerate temperatures well below freezing—check with your local nursery regarding hardiness for your particular location.

Sedum acre is fast-growing and spreads quickly, with yellow flowers; *S. lydium* is a dwarf creeper with red-tipped leaves and white or pink flowers; and *S. sieboldii* is a pink-flowered trailer with 1-inch, round leaves. The Mexican sedum (*Sedum amecamecanum*) is a good, yellow-flowered choice in cool-summer climates; for small areas, *S. rubrotinctum* will cover the ground quickly with bronze-tinted leaves that resemble jelly beans. *S. spathulifolium*, with its blue green rosettes on short, trailing stems, weaves in and out of crevices as an exciting rock garden possibility.

Dudleyas, sempervivums, aeoniums, and echeverias also have species that make good ground covers. Mix them or match them, or plant an entire area with just one kind—the contrasts in color and form are numerous. *Dudleya candida, Echeveria elegans, Aeonium decorum,* and *Sempervivum tectorum* are among the most popular species.

Ice plants

Undoubtedly, the succulents earning the best reputation as first-class ground covers are the ice plants. Called mesembryanthemums (see page 51 and opposite page), they are often sold by genera.

Most are low-growing (to about 9 inches high) with bright, daisy-shaped flowers in many sizes and all colors but blue. They provide a showy display in spring or summer, and attractive foliage throughout the year. On overcast days, flowers close, but in sun they present a vivid carpet of color that is seen for miles.

Besides being decorative, many species provide excellent erosion control on fairly steep slopes, and because of their fleshy foliage, they are about as fire-resistant as plants can be. Their main drawback is a lack of winter hardiness that limits outdoor usefulness to mild-winter climates where they are considered perennials. Most species, though, are colorful and attractive enough to be used as container plants in northern climates where low temperatures otherwise would limit their use in permanent landscapes.

Shopping for ice plants can be bewildering. Nurseries offer many kinds and some are labeled only according to flower color. Try to imagine how an ice plant will look out of bloom. Some flower spectacularly, and then have nondescript foliage the rest of the year. Consider, too, whether you're going to plant a slope or flat ground. Small-leafed or trailing types provide much better erosion control on hillsides than big-leafed or clumping types. If you plan to grow them only in containers, then the amount of colorful flowers will be your main concern.

Though ice plants are considered drought-resistant, they can't survive without any irrigation except near the ocean where fog provides moisture. Inland gardeners need to water ice plant ground covers—in hot areas, possibly as much as once a week.

Descriptive List of Ice Plants

Kind of Ice Plant	In Bloom	Out of Bloom	Uses
Red Spike Ice Plant *Cephalophyllum* 'Red Spike' (often sold as *Cylindrophyllum speciosum*)	Brilliant early show of 2-inch cerise blooms, January to March	Pointed, gray green leaves stick straight up. Plant forms clump 3–5 inches high	Use in small areas—along border, in parking strip, as pattern plant. Clumpy plants don't spread much, provide little erosion protection. Space 6 inches apart so plants fill in thickly
White Trailing Ice Plant *Delosperma* 'Alba'	Scattering of small white flowers never amounts to much	Good dark green all year. Plants spread low, form sturdy 6–8-inch mat. Leaves are an inch long	First-rate for covering steep slopes or level ground. Runners spread rapidly, root, knit together to form strong, hill-holding network. Doesn't get woody or mound up. Foliage texture suits big or small areas
Rosea Ice Plant *Drosanthemum floribundum* and *D. hispidum*	Tiny but incredibly profuse flowers bloom in dazzling sheets, late spring and early summer. Pink to purple	Tiny, glistening, gray green leaves. Long trailing stems root, form spongy, 6–8-inch mat	Lightweight, easy to root, can cling to steepest, rockiest slopes, can drape several feet over a wall. Also makes neat lawn substitute. One way to plant: just crumble or chop up stems, broadcast like seeds, cover with sand
Bush-Type Ice Plant *Lampranthus aurantiacus*	Brilliant flowers bloom early and heavily. Varieties are 'Glaucus' (yellow), 'Gold Nugget' (orange), 'Sunman' (gold)	Clumpy, erect plants look like foot-tall shrubs. Gray green 2-inch leaves	For low borders, gentle slopes, or where you'd use any dwarf flowering shrub. Clumpy growth makes it unsuitable for erosion control. Space 6 inches apart for quick, solid fill, Shearing in summer makes the planting neater
Purple Ice Plant *Lampranthus productus*	Vivid purple flowers come in sheets early, last long. Can bloom before Christmas, last till May	Small, bronze-tipped leaves form solid 15-inch-high cover	Best on level areas, moderate slopes. Half-trailing, half-clumping plants don't provide dependable erosion control on steep banks
Trailing Ice Plant *Lampranthus spectabilis*	Spectacular flowers but season is short, dead flowers messy. Available in pink, rose pink, purple, red	Foliage never looks rich like some ice plants. Small gray green leaves. Plants trail, grow foot tall. Pink variety has best foliage	Flowers alone justify planting, but it is also trustworthy ground cover on all but biggest, steepest slopes. Grow it where off-season untidiness won't be prominent
Croceum Ice Plant *Malephora crocea* **Yellow Trailing Ice Plant** *M. luteola*	Sparse but long-blooming. *M. crocea* is reddish yellow; *M.c. purpureo-crocea*, salmon; *M. luteola*, yellow	Attractive year-round foliage. *M. luteola* has finer texture, best all-year foliage of ice plants	Popular freeway plants. Handsome ground covers for small or large flat areas, moderately steep slopes. *M. crocea* works on hillsides better than *M. luteola*, which doesn't send out long runners

(both often sold as *Hymenocyclus*)

Permanent landscapes

Just because you want to include cacti and succulents in the landscape doesn't mean the entire area must contain them. Some of the most distinctive combinations of succulents and other plants are shown on the following pages.

During spring and summer, heat-loving annuals and perennials offer spectacular colors that complement the bold forms of some succulent plants. Succulents can also be used as borders or edgings around the base of trees and shrubs. In many cases, unsightly roots that pop through cracked topsoil can be camouflaged with a carpet of low-growing succulents.

If you do wish to plant a garden of succulents and cacti exclusively, start with the larger, background plants—they become the frame for your landscape picture. Torch cacti, yuccas, aloes, and agaves are good candidates for this. An authentic desert scene can be achieved with the addition of groups of rocks. Along with standard, heavier rocks, you can also buy lava rock and feather rock from building supply yards and some garden centers. Plant around rocks with medium-size plants; in between with smaller kinds.

Because all succulents—especially cacti—need perfect drainage, a raised bed or sloped area is an ideal location for them. On level or nearly level ground where soil is any texture but light, dig a deep planting hole (at least 2 feet deep) and replace the excavated soil with a light, gritty or sandy soil mixture (see page 75). After planting, cover the soil with a thin layer of crushed gravel or pebbles around the roots of the plant for frost protection.

Cacti and succulents raised outdoors take more water in summer than many gardeners realize. Because of cooler temperatures in spring and autumn, plants don't need as much supplementary water as in summer. Where summers remain rainless, it is possible that some plants will require a weekly watering.

During autumn and winter, when plants need to rest, it is important to reduce the amount of water they receive. This helps them to harden and withstand lower temperatures. It is not only cold that can damage plants; wet soil is another condition which also makes the first freeze hazardous.

Because of many factors—age of plant, location in the garden, soil, and moisture—it is difficult to determine the degree of hardiness for each individual cactus and succulent. In our plant selection chapters we suggest the minimum temperatures at which most species will remain healthy. Whenever possible, buy plants from local nurseries and garden centers because you can be reasonably sure they will survive in your area.

If you live in an area where below-freezing weather occurs in winter, it is still possible to have succulents and cacti in outdoor gardens—just keep them in pots. During warmer months, you can sink the pots in the ground in your permanent landscape; then when freezing temperatures threaten in autumn, plants can be returned to cool, indoor shelter for the winter.

This list of cacti and succulents features bold or unusually shaped plants around which you can build a landscape.

Agaves: *A. americana, A. attenuata, A. filifera, A. parrasana*
Aloes: *A. arborescens, A. striata*
Carnegiea: *C. gigantea*
Cephalocereus: *C. fulviceps, C. palmeri*
Cereus: *C. hildmannianus, C. peruvianus*
Cleistocactus: *C. baumanii, C. strausii*
Echinocactus: *E. grusonii, E. ingens*
Echinocereus: *E. enneacanthus, E. pectinatus, E. reichenbachii*
Euphorbias: *E. grandicornis, E. ingens*
Ferocactus: *F. acanthodes, F. wislizenii*
Kalanchoes: *K. beharensis*
Lemaireocereus: *L. marginatus, L. thurberi*
Opuntias: *O. basilaris, O. bigelovii, O. ficus-indica, O. microdasys, O. prolifera*
Trichocereus: *T. peruvianus, T. spachianus*
Yuccas: *Y. aloifolia, Y. brevifolia, Y. elephantipes, Y. glauca, Y. whipplei*

Desert rock gardens

Many desert gardeners, eager to use their natural surroundings to the fullest, have developed freeform planting areas that feature cacti and succulents exclusively. (See photograph at lower right, on opposite page.) More than a simple rock garden, these interestingly shaped areas combine natural stones, pieces of wood, and other elements with plants to create miniature desert landscapes.

It may be possible to take advantage of natural garden contours—slight hillside slopes, ravines, or areas near boulders or other large rocks. The most important factors to consider when selecting a location are good exposure and well-draining soil: areas with east, west, or south-facing exposures that blend into the existing garden naturally are good choices. Take a little time to arrange plants carefully, giving special consideration to their shape, foliage color and texture, and rate of growth.

Plant them in patterns

Here's an eye-catching but far less elaborate adaptation of Victorian planting beds and perennial borders—a patterned succulent bed. We mentioned that many low-growing succulents and cacti have distinctive leaf shapes, colors, or forms. Some ambitious gardeners take full advantage of these plants by artistically arranging them in beds so that intricate and colorful patterns can be seen. Symmetrical succulents like rosette-forming aeoniums, echeverias, sempervivums, and others are particular favorites for such planting beds, as are the rounded cacti—echinopsis, mammillarias, and many ball and barrel species.

Landscaping

Striking, bold shape of tall cereus combines attractively with flowering native shrubs, perennials, other succulents. Planting area is protected by house from burning desert sun in afternoon. Design: Lou Gerlach.

Low-growing echeveria rosettes circle base of tree, holding soil in place and covering unsightly roots. Framed living mural of succulents (directions for making one are on page 67) hangs on fence.

Year after year, *Trichocereus schickendantzii* is crowned with dozens of canary yellow blooms that appear at night, close the following morning.

Rock-lined, raised planting bed makes handsome display for collection of prized cacti. Plants receive occasional maintenance, full sun throughout year.

More Landscaping

Charming vignette of lush mosses, grasses, and succulents includes (clockwise) Blue fescue,
Sedum spathulifolium, Cotyledon tomentosa, tiny sedums, Scotch moss, *Echeveria glauca,* juniper.

Hardy Trichocereus species is excellent
outdoor subject. Fragrant, 10-inch-long
flowers appear in early summer.

Blooming *Echinopsis multiplex* and *Notocactus leninghausii* planted in soil-filled drainage tiles. Lavender flowers are delicately scented, appear profusely in late spring.

Blooming hillside retaining wall has levels planted with drought-resistant succulents. Crassulas, echeverias, sedums, ice plants, opuntia create patchwork of color throughout spring.

Dazzling display of color from daisylike ice plant flowers. Spring, summer-blooming species are quick growers, flower freely in mild-winter areas.

Special Displays

Cascading branches of carefully pruned *Portulacaria afra variegata* resemble living sculpture when displayed on wooden pedestal.

Terra cotta strawberry jar has individual planting pockets, ideal for showing off prized succulents. Small, rosette-forming species grow in side pockets; tall, *Crassula falcata* from the top.

Wood platforms, constructed of lath strips and mounted on support beams, make striking displays for special potted favorites.

Handsome display for cactus collection is made of redwood lumber, heavy-duty chain. Holes are drilled through boards, and chain is threaded through holes; narrow dowels, fitted through chain links, hold shelves at desired level.

Special plants need special displays

When your cacti and succulents have a special feature, give them a chance to perform. Place them where everyone who passes can appreciate them—most of all, make sure that you will enjoy them many times during each day.

Why not set aside a special area for a prized cactus collection, or display a special plant on a pedestal as you would a piece of sculpture? If your favorite plant has unusual form or foliage, set it off dramatically against a plain wall or fence.

You can easily transform a monotonous wall or the side of a house into a show place for a collection of container plants. The lower left photo on the opposite page shows how one cactus collector solved the dilemma of too many potted plants. Holes are drilled into 1-by-12 redwood boards; then ordinary chain is threaded through. Narrow dowels, cut about 2 inches long, go through the links, holding the shelves in place at the desired level.

Balcony (or patio overhang) support beams are usually just 4-by-4 posts, and unless disguised in some way, they can be quite unattractive. Consider giving these posts a double purpose by making them into a display structure for potted plants (see photo below right on opposite page). Platforms of varying sizes are constructed of ½ by 2-inch lath strips, then positioned on support posts at different levels—that way, you can accommodate almost any size plant. Containers remove easily both for watering and plant maintenance.

Espaliers

Unsightly empty spaces, either along a fence or against a bare wall, can be dressed up with climbing or trailing succulents. Suggesting a bit of the tropics, many established plants cover an entire area with a profusion of colorful blooms each year. Fine species like night-blooming cereus, epiphyllums, and other vining types, can be loosely trained into attractive espaliers supported on a trellis or attached directly to the wall or fence.

In tropical areas where temperatures don't drop below 40°F., night-blooming cereus (*Hylocereus undatus*) is an easy-to-grow species with bright green stems and enormous, white, nocturnal flowers. In many tropical regions it is trained into hedges, but consider it, too, for an espalier against a wall. You may want to plant it close to a bedroom window—a subtle fragrance fills the air on warm summer nights. Other vining plants include *Selenicereus macdonaldiae* (queen of the night) and *S. pteranthus* (princess of the night).

Living murals

Living murals—succulents rooted and grown in soil that is held behind a chicken wire frame—offer an exciting way to display favorite succulent plants. A long, narrow box (4 by 1½ feet by 8 inches is a good size), resembling an empty picture frame with a bottom, is covered with chicken wire that has been stretched, and then stapled into position. The box is filled and planted while on the ground, then tilted and hung once plants are established.

Here's how to make a mural of your own: Fill the box with lightweight potting soil, packing it so that the soil doesn't settle when the box is tilted on edge. Cover the soil with an inch of green moss; then stretch 1-inch-mesh chicken wire over it and staple down. Plant full-grown succulents or cuttings directly into the soil; after they have taken root (3–6 weeks), hang the mural on a fence or patio wall. You can water gently by spraying the mural or through holes drilled in the top (water trickles down the full depth of the box).

When shopping for succulents to use in a wall-hung mural, look for low-growing types like small aeoniums, crassulas, echeverias, sedums, sempervivums, and similar mat-forming or rosette types.

Hanging succulents

Gracefully cascading over the edge of a container, hanging succulents and cacti are bound to attract attention. There are many fine succulent plants suitable for hanging baskets that offer a handsome display of flowers and foliage.

One of the most popular house plants, *Sedum morganianum* (donkey tail), has overlapping, fleshy leaves that trail down stems, sometimes 4 feet or more. Another favorite group, the schlumbergera hybrids (Christmas cactus), make quite a colorful display of red blooms in late autumn. The *Hylocereus* and *Selenicereus* species are, by their nature, pendant growers, but since they become quite large at maturity, young plants are the most suitable for hanging baskets.

Trailing crassulas, sedums, and some mesembryanthemums each offer something unique when suspended at eye level. *Crassula perforata* (necklace vine) has pairs of blue gray leaves marked with tiny red dots; *C. schmidtii* produces tiny, light pink flowers throughout spring. Besides donkey tail sedum, other species include these: *Sedum brevifolium,* with its tiny, waxy white, round leaves; *S. sieboldii,* with notched blue gray leaves and pink flowers; and *S. stahlii* with greenish-brown foliage and yellow flowers.

Succulent plants in hanging containers need a somewhat moist soil, especially when grown outdoors during the warm summer months. Wire-framed baskets lined with sphagnum moss and filled with soil are particularly susceptible to drying out—you may need to water them as often as every other day. When planting a basket such as this, use several plants of the same kind for a lavish display, or try mixing them (see page 54 for ideas about hanging dish gardens). To look their best, baskets should be full, almost brimming over.

Two points to remember before hanging a plant are the strength of the supporting structure and the location's exposure to elements like sun, shade, and wind. Because a 12-inch wooden box or wire basket weighs as much as 30 pounds—even more when wet—test your support structure well before suspending any hanging container.

Tips for Easy Care

We're calling this section "Tips for Easy Care" for a good reason: raising cacti and succulents is less work than gardening with most other plants. Their fleshy stems and leaves are able to store great quantities of water—helpful if you forget to tend them. Their tough or spiny exterior is rarely attacked by insects—it is just too hard. And if you do mistreat a plant, you'll discover it has tremendous recuperative powers.

Lack of attention is not the way to successfully grow cacti and succulents, and in no way are we suggesting you neglect your plants. Just remember that succulents have endured tremendously adverse conditions along the way; yet they remain hardy, adaptive, always intriguing—true survivors of our changing environment.

The right location makes the difference

Because cacti and succulents are so intriguing, many collectors submit to the temptation of buying too many plants, and then find themselves without adequate room. To compensate for the lack of growing space, a few unfortunate plants are relocated to less-favorable environments. Inevitably, this leads to disappointment—the plants languish and soon die, hidden away in dark or shaded areas.

Though optimum conditions are always desirable, some plants will—if they must—adjust to less-than-ideal conditions. In such situations, plants will not grow as well or bloom as profusely as you might like, but they will survive. Light affects the color of foliage and the formation of flower buds. In sun, leaves have a strong color and there is abundant bloom; in dim light, plants are somewhat less colorful and flowering sparse.

So before you set out to buy any plant, take a little time to decide just where it will go. The right location *does* make all the difference.

Indoors

Indoors, a window receiving indirect sun or bright light is generally best for cacti and succulents. Tender

plants—rebutias, epiphyllums, some young succulents—should be protected from harsh sunlight to avoid burning their outer skin. Turn potted plants occasionally so that all parts of the plant receive an equal amount of light. The exceptions to this are tender cacti and plants that are about to bloom: do not move them—change in light could cause buds to drop.

Rather than placing a few plants at several different windows, try putting them all in one area; it will be easier to water them and keep them groomed. If you want plants to accent a shaded area, the addition of artificial light is needed. Or, if you have an unusual, specimen-size plant in a handsome container, place it in a well-lighted spot for a dramatic interior accent. Just be sure it is not in a heavily traveled area. As striking as many large cacti are, they can be incredibly wicked if bumped into.

Outdoors

Be somewhat careful when selecting plants that will be grown outdoors. Usually, local nurseries will stock plants suitable for local climatic conditions. If you're not sure that the plants are hardy enough for your climate, though, don't put them in the ground; grow them in containers for awhile. If necessary, they can be moved inside or to a protected area when frost threatens. Of course, you can experiment, too. A great number of succulents and cacti will tolerate cool nights and temperatures close to freezing.

Under artificial sunshine

Where natural light is limited or nonexistent, you can still grow healthy, handsome indoor plants by using artificial light overhead. Fluorescent and incandescent lights are not by themselves miracle workers; plants still require attention—perhaps even more care than they do on windowsills. Plain fluorescent lights can supply sufficient light for plant growth; incandescent lights cannot—they are not strong enough in the red and blue color bands that plants need, and they generate too much heat for many sensitive plants.

Under artificial lights plants grow all year. Because a vital part of succulent and cacti growing involves allowing plants to rest at proper times, some mature plants dislike the year-round growth period under lights. If you're an experienced grower, you probably can handle mature specimens successfully this way, but the beginner would be wise to experiment first with smaller plants before risking the investment in money and years of growth that many large specimens represent.

It is important to distribute the light evenly over plants. Remember that the light is strongest at the center of the tube. Several fluorescent tubes placed side by side are best, though one tube alone usually will support plant life that depends solely on this light. Reflectors or canopies painted white help to distribute light by "throwing it back" on to plants. You can use standard industrial fixtures (from electrical suppliers) or commercial plant stands with adjustable reflectors (available at plant suppliers). With both fixtures you slip the tubes in place and you're ready to grow.

There are a number of prefabricated light-reflector–plant tray combinations that you can purchase, ranging in size from two-lamp table models to floor carts with several shelves. Whether you purchase one of these lighting units or make one, be sure to provide some method of adjusting the shelf height to allow for plant growth and variety of container size. Start with the tubes 6–12 inches above the plants. If new growth seems to bunch together unnaturally, plants are getting too much light; if they become leggy, they need more light. Because fluorescent lighting will not harm plants, lights may be set as close as needed.

What to look for

Because of the overwhelming variety of cacti and succulents, you should know something about them before you shop for plants. Take a look at the illustrations and photographs in this book and decide which plants appeal to you most. Some are truly outstanding, many are more bizarre than beautiful, and a few, admittedly, are just weird. That's what is unique about the entire succulent family—you can find something for everyone.

Look for specimens with good color and form, abundant bloom, and vigorous growth. You may want to ask if the plants were grown from seed or cuttings (this can affect hardiness), or, in some cases, field collected. Though most people start collections with whatever plants appeal to them, sooner or later some find a particular group that interests them more than others.

Flower shows, especially those sponsored by cacti and succulent societies, contain displays of plants that will help acquaint you with the variety of flowers and plants available. Often scheduled in spring and summer months when plants are in bloom, these shows let you see hundreds of species at one time.

When you shop for plants

Local nurseries have become aware of the rise in popularity of both cacti and succulents and now offer more of a selection. Though these plants are generally small, they are excellent for beginners or for those who enjoy watching their plants grow over the years.

Besides local nurseries and garden centers, succulent plants are available at specialty nurseries (limited to just cacti and succulents), from mail-order suppliers, and from friends. If you have the chance to visit a specialty nursery, do so—even if you're just looking. Along with expert advice you'll find a wide assortment of common and rare plants in all sizes from tiny year-old seedlings to full-grown, mature specimens.

If you order plants by mail, start with just a few; when they prove satisfactory, you can order more with confidence. Most collectors find mail-order suppliers to be very reputable, offering only healthy, well-established plants. Often, the stock comes in pots in which the plants have long been established before shipment. In comparison, bargain counters at dime stores and supermarkets can be a gamble: usually plants sold here are newly collected or recently replanted and are going through a critical adjustment period under unfavorable conditions. Such plants may be difficult for you to establish successfully.

If you plan to landscape with succulents, you may choose to buy larger plants. The safest, least expensive way to ship plants is bare root (without soil). Almost all cacti and succulents are sent this way because there is less chance of damage—this plus the fact that shipping costs would otherwise be prohibitive. Also, too much humidity in the soil could cause rot if the shipment was delayed. Upon arrival, bare root plants can be potted in regular soil mix, but you should wait about a week before watering.

For long or cross-country distances, have plants sent Priority or Express Mail (air freight), but for shorter trips, shipment by ground transportation is satisfactory. In most cases, you'll have to go to the freight companies to retrieve your plants. Remember, it is better to get them immediately—a few days' wait can be dangerous.

Spring and autumn are the best times to buy plants from mail-order suppliers, though most of them do ship bare root plants throughout the year, using more protective packing in winter and midsummer.

Handling new arrivals

When new plants arrive, either from a local nursery or by mail, they need more care in the first few weeks than at any other time. It is in these first weeks that plants must adapt to new conditions, and if you're not careful, the transition can be more of a shock than an adjustment.

Plants that have traveled for any length of time in closed boxes should not be put immediately in direct sunlight—it could easily damage or burn their sensitive skin. Instead, find a spot that's indirectly lighted. After a few days they can be moved again, this time to a place that gets more light.

When you receive plants in the mail, even from the most reputable supplier, check to see that they are free from insects. Even the most regulated nurseries have their share of pests. You may be surprised to see how

selecting

Row after row of grafted cacti—*Rebutia heliosa (Aylostera)* in foreground, *Rebutia nivea*—grown in 4-inch pots, are raised in greenhouse, later sold on premises.

Mature, field-grown specimens of *Agave baha parrasana* (foreground) and *Echinocactus grusonii* are dug up, potted when sold.

Colorful ice plants (mesembryanthemums) are sold in flats as well as individual pots. Hardy, sprawling species will cling to steep, rocky slopes or spread as indestructible ground covers. Vibrant, daisylike blooms are available in all colors but blue.

many unexpected visitors appear on the soil surface when you immerse the pot halfway in a tub of water. So before new arrivals officially join the rest of your collection, it is important to thoroughly examine each one. (See page 76 for a few painless ways to handle cacti without getting stuck.)

If you choose NOT to buy

One of the most fascinating things about succulent plants is the ease with which one can propagate them. It is not only easy but fun to increase the number of plants you have by using one of these methods: grafting, cuttings or offsets, or seed.

Each method has its advantages. Grafting plants such as cacti is an exciting yet simple way of combining two plants to grow as one, and the result is often a healthier specimen. Taking cuttings or offsets—parts of stems, leaves, branches—for new plants is the easiest and perhaps the most successful way to propagate. There is no waiting years for growth and bloom; some species started from cuttings become blooming plants in just a few months. Though much slower, sowing seeds is economical and you often get more plants than you expected. The stock is usually clean and free of pests. The only way to be guaranteed of growing a true form of a plant is to raise it from a cutting.

Grafting—from two you get one

Grafting offers you the opportunity to combine plant forms not found in nature, and often your imagination is the only limitation to your creativity. The gang on the next page—we consider them a very special group of

grafting

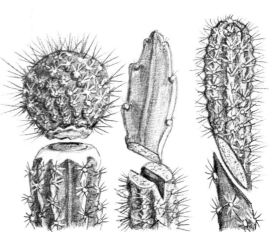

1. Slice off top of stock plant. A second, very thin slice may be made and left in place to keep cut surface moist.

2. Flat graft (left) is best for rounded scions; cleft graft (center) for flat-scion species like epiphyllums; side graft (right) for long, slender scions.

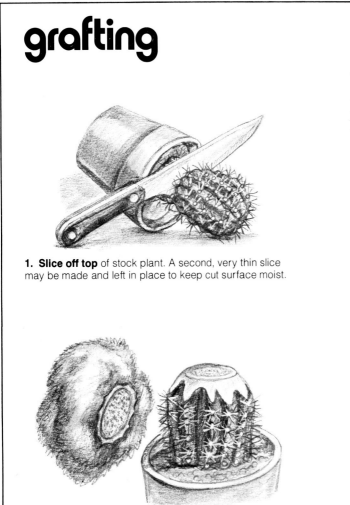

3. After trimming down edges of stock, match it with scion so both diameters are same size; if not matched, graft will fail to unite.

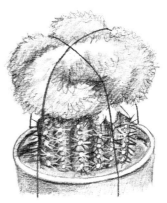

4. Remove thin, protective slice (step 1) and quickly apply scion; press them gently together. Secure scion in place with rubber bands.

The grafted gang: (from left) *Rebutia nivea, Gymnocalycium venturianum, Sulcorebutia glomerseta, Lobivia* hybrid, *Espostoa mirabilis, Gymnocalycium* (ruby ball graft), and *Rebutia heliosa* (*Aylostera*).

cacti—were propagated by grafting for various reasons.

This technique can be used to create or preserve plant oddities like crests and other unusual shapes, and it is also a way of getting difficult plants to take root. For example, the top of a damaged (but healthy) cactus can be transplanted to a stronger base stock and will continue to grow—though its appearance may change—just as before. You'll discover, too, that grafted subjects frequently grow more quickly and vigorously than those propagated from cuttings.

Unfortunately, not all succulents can be grafted; only members of the cactus, milkweed, and euphorbia families have the essential cambium or growth layer to be successful candidates. It is the growth layer, right underneath the epidermis, that transfers water and nutrients throughout the entire plant.

The best time to graft is during the growing season—from May to October—when plants are strong and have enough sap flowing to ensure a perfect union of all parts.

There are three grafting methods: flat, cleft, and side. The **flat graft**—fitting a flat base to a flat top—is easiest and especially good when you are working with rounded scions (the *scion* is the piece that is to be grafted). After selecting the understock, make a cut straight across on each plant with a clean, sharp knife. Since cacti have a hard, waxy epidermis, bevel the edges of both stock and scion to prevent shrinkage (see illustration on opposite page). Press the two flat surfaces together and secure with rubber bands, string, or toothpicks.

The **cleft graft** fits a wedge-shaped base into a "v" cut. Plants with flat scions like epiphyllums should be cleft-grafted. Join the two pieces with a toothpick or tie them with string.

The last method is a **side graft**, in which both plants are cut on a slant and respective pieces joined with string until a union is formed. Long slender scions are best handled with a side graft. In all methods, the grafted union should be held firmly but gently in place.

It is vital to the success of the graft that the understock be healthy because it must support the scion until it is ready to grow on its own. Therefore, be sure to select plump, fresh plants and scions from firm growing tips or new offshoots. It is also important to fit the cut surfaces together evenly so that the growth layer of both parts will be in contact. Try to keep cuts free of dirt and dust. If running sap becomes a problem, soak the parts in water for a few minutes (to dissolve sap) and blot dry.

A few postoperative days of partial shade will help your recuperating plant. Check occasionally to be sure the rubber bands or strings are not too tight. Spines or toothpicks used to secure graft unions should be removed in about a week; they last for years and can be a source of infection if left indefinitely.

It is interesting to observe how grafted plants change in appearance once they are being fed by a new understock. Some become bloated and produce a great many young offsets, but this does not alter their botanical status; they always retain their original classifica-tion, though many receive a more complicated new name. On the opposite page, the little one in the front row with the yellow flowers in her bonnet is really called *Sulcorebutia glomerseta*.

New plants from seed

If you plan to grow many seedlings, sow seeds in wooden boxes or nursery flats; for small quantities of seed, you can use shallow pots (bulb or azalea pots are fine). Start seeds in spring or early summer so they have a chance to grow before cold weather arrives. A suitable growing mix combines equal parts of loose topsoil or planting mix, leaf mold, and coarse sand or fine gravel. You can also use a commercial artificial medium like vermiculite in place of sand. It is important to keep the potting mix loose rather than packed down in the container and to leave sufficient room at the top for watering.

An easy rule to follow when sowing seeds is to bury them at a depth twice their own diameter. Large seeds can be set in place by hand; smaller ones, like those from crassulas and cotyledons, should be sprinkled on the surface of the dampened soil and covered with a thin layer of coarse sand or fine gravel. Place the seed pans in a warm, bright location (without direct sun) and cover them with newspaper or a sheet of glass. This provides a humid atmosphere that keeps the soil moist and warm enough for germination. Whenever the cover sweats, allow some air into the container; you should keep the temperature fairly constant (65°F. is good) and the pots out of drafts.

The easiest method of watering is to set the seed pot in a pan of water and let the water soak up into the soil. If you prefer to water from above, be sure to use a fine, soft-spray mist; otherwise seeds might be disturbed and possibly "washed out." It is important to keep de-

collecting

After cactus blooms, remaining fruit (seed pod) becomes swollen, filled with soft pulp. Seeds inside are scattered throughout; they can be collected, dried, stored for future planting.

propagating

Leaf cuttings: Cut fleshy leaves into small pieces, mark which edge is up, and let dry for a week. Insert—bottom edge down—in potting mix.

Division: Clumping or rosette-forming succulents can be divided into individual plants; each crown will root, become nucleus of new clump.

Offsets: Young cactus offsets at base of larger plant can be carefully separated, rooted in sandy mix; each offset will grow into separate cactus.

Leaf cuttings: Either entire leaf or a part of one are removed, allowed to dry (callus) a few days; then rooted.

veloping seedlings evenly moist: too much moisture brings on mildew; too little water and the plants will perish.

Germination—the sprouting of the seeds—depends on many factors: temperature, soil moisture, and climate. Seeds are different and there is a considerable variation in the time it takes each one to germinate. For example, stapelias sprout in a few days, while some cacti take a whole year.

Once your seeds germinate

Once seeds have successfully germinated—true leaves are apparent and seedlings are about ¼ inch high—remove the covering to give the new plants a little more light. Air and light are vital factors now. Too much air and light can cause seedlings to burn and turn reddish or bronze colored; too little air and light causes them to become pale or yellow, and often a fungus forms which eventually rots the new plant.

New seedlings are fragile, so when you transplant them from their original containers, *handle with care*. A section of tiny plants may be pried up and then carefully separated with tweezers. Always handle seedlings by their leaves (if any) rather than by the stems to avoid damage.

New plants from cuttings

As the illustrations above show, cacti and succulents can be propagated in various ways. In the most common method, **stem cuttings** are taken from the stem tip or from a section of stem that contains leaf nodes. **Leaf cuttings** can be used too—either a whole leaf or only part of one. First, dry the leaf for a few days; then place it in a light, sandy soil. Gasterias, crassulas, kalanchoes, and haworthias are good plants to propagate by leaf cuttings.

Taking **offsets**—small plantlets that appear on flower stalks or at the base of larger plants—is another way to propagate. Aloes, agaves, haworthias, echeverias, and crassulas produce offsets that can be pulled off from the "mother" plant and rooted.

Plants that form clumps of many crowns—echeverias, aeoniums, many cacti—can be pulled off or severed with a knife (if plants are cut, they should be dried off in a shady spot for a week) and then planted. This method is called **division** and requires the same growth treatment as taking offsets: a damp, sandy rooting mix, even moisture, and a shady location.

Soil mixes

Contrary to popular belief, cacti and succulents DO NOT grow in pure sand; they require good, nutritious soil. Every grower undoubtedly has a favorite recipe, and what works well for one may not work well for another. For example, climate plays a part in the choice of soils. In weather that's consistently warm, a loose, well-drained mixture may be good if you water regularly, whereas a heavier soil may be better when plants are not watered as often.

Here is a satisfactory growing mix for most succulents: combine equal parts of loose soil or potting mix, leaf mold, and coarse sand. For cacti, add more sand and some fine gravel to the mix. Tree-dwelling, tropical species of epiphyllum and rhipsalis thrive in a richer mixture: combine equal parts of shredded fir bark or osmunda (available at nurseries) and loose soil or potting mix. In all cases, the mixes should be thoroughly blended and have a loose texture. This guarantees your plants a fast-draining, moisture-retaining soil.

Prepared soil mixes (not packaged), available at most nurseries and garden centers, contain the necessary nutrients for good plant growth. They also have been sterilized so there is little chance of weeds or bacteria appearing. Prepackaged potting mixes—usually available in 1 or 2-cubic-foot bags—need more sand to be suitable for desert plants. Soil-less or peat-like mixes, though lightweight and good for many plants, are inappropriate except when used as a propagating medium. They lack any nutrients, and cacti and succulents planted in them require a careful feeding program to remain healthy.

Which container is best?

Clay or plastic pots, wooden boxes, nursery flats, even pieces of rock can be suitable containers for growing cacti and succulents. The only prerequisite is that they provide good drainage so that soil is kept loose and well aerated.

The familiar terra cotta (red clay) pot is the most popular choice. It is relatively inexpensive and comes in many sizes, but because it is made of a porous material, plants dry out faster. On the other hand, plants grown in glazed pots must be watered with more caution because moisture cannot escape through the pot's sides.

Plastic pots are often used because they are neat, inexpensive, colorful, and lightweight—an important

Ouch!

Experienced cactus growers know—though often they learned a little late—just how to handle the prickly ones. They know that whether you are transplanting, grooming, or merely rearranging pots of cacti, if you're not careful, it is easy to wind up with a handful of spiny bristles.

For those who have never handled cacti before and want some preventive tips — even for those who are experienced—here are a few painless ways to avoid getting stuck:

1) When potting or repotting, fashion a thick newspaper handle, wrap it around the cactus stem about halfway up, and gently lift the plant out of the pot. Or turn the pot on its side, make a sling out of folded-up newspaper, surround the cactus, and grasp the paper tightly at the top. Slide the pot backwards off the rootball.

2) When adding soil, keep fingers away from bristles by making a newspaper funnel or chute; let the soil slide down around the roots.

3) If something falls into your cactus—leaves, twigs, bits of paper—and you want to remove it, find a pair of long-handled wooden or metal tongs. For stubborn debris, use a vacuum cleaner fitted with a narrow furniture attachment.

4) General grooming to remove dust, dirt, or cobwebs can be done gently with a whisk broom or any other soft-bristled brush or with a spray of water. Protect your hands with gloves.

If you do get stuck, a piece of cellophane tape will pull out a few small bristles. If you really get stuck with a handful of painless bristles, apply a thin coat of rubber cement. Let it dry; then rub it off. Bristles come out easily.

consideration if you plan to hang your plant. They have a tendency to tip over, though, if they contain large specimens, or blow over in gusty winds if plants are small.

When selecting a container, consider the size of the plant in relation to its prospective home. Not only does a small plant look lost in a large pot, it rarely thrives because unused soil tends to become waterlogged. Conversely, you can't expect a large specimen to respond for very long to the cramped quarters of a tiny pot.

For round plants—ball or barrel cacti or clustering succulents—use a pot 1 or 2 inches wider than the diameter of the plant. For vertical plants, like torch cacti, euphorbias, and aloes, choose a pot half as wide as the plant is tall. Remember that small pots under 4 inches wide are hard to care for; they dry out rapidly and plants always seem to need water.

potting

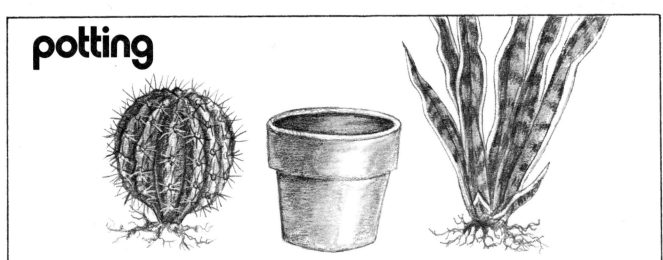

A good rule of thumb to follow when selecting containers: rounded cacti need a container only 2 inches greater in diameter than that of the plant; vertical cacti or other succulents are best planted in containers having a diameter half the height of the plant.

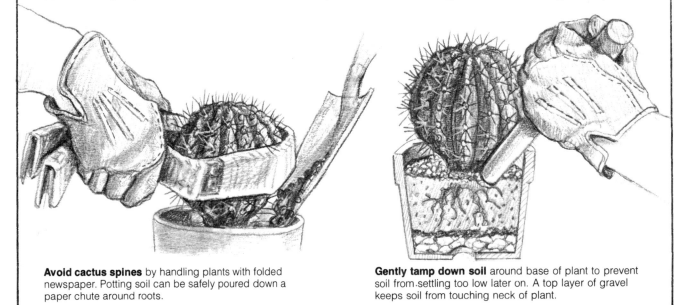

Avoid cactus spines by handling plants with folded newspaper. Potting soil can be safely poured down a paper chute around roots.

Gently tamp down soil around base of plant to prevent soil from settling too low later on. A top layer of gravel keeps soil from touching neck of plant.

Tips on potting and repotting

Before you plant in a used pot or box, take the trouble to scrub it well with hot water (add ½ cup household bleach per gallon of water) and a brush. This eliminates any pests and diseases that may have been left by previous plants and soil. If your container is porous, soak it in water before you plant so it won't absorb moisture from the potting mix.

Cover the pot's drainage hole with a curved shard of pottery, stones, or a square of fine-mesh wire screen to prevent clogging and minimize soil loss. If you have a decorative container with no drainage hole, you can plant your succulent or cactus in an ordinary clay pot that fits inside the more attractive container. Just make sure when you water, that the bottom of the clay pot isn't left sitting in water.

Because succulents are susceptible to rot from excessive moisture, check to see that the soil mix is fairly dry before potting your plant. Put a small mound of soil in the container, to a depth of 2 inches or so, and center the plant. If the plant is too high, take some soil out; if too low, add more soil. Fill in and around the roots with soil until the container is almost full, leaving room for water. Settle the mix by rapping the bottom of the pot gently, but don't pack the mix tightly in place.

For species that are especially sensitive to excessive moisture, a top layer of gravel can be added to prevent the base of the plant from coming in contact with the potting soil.

Do not water newly potted plants immediately. Allow plants to dry for several days and then water sparingly for the first few weeks. This allows time for any broken roots to heal.

Repotting is best done in mild weather months when plants have a chance to grow without being threatened by severe temperatures.

First, see if the plant will *easily* pull out of its container. If it doesn't, *don't force it.* Hold the pot upside down, rap the side sharply against a table edge, and let the plant fall gently from the pot. The idea is to get the plant free with the root ball intact. Gently crumble some of the old soil from the roots. The less shock a plant receives, the better it will adjust to transplanting.

Look for the "soil level" mark on your plant—this indicates how deep the plant grew in its original soil. Try to avoid repotting deeper than that mark to discourage any chance of rotting. If you're unsure where the soil level mark is, add a top layer of gravel.

When a plant and container refuse to separate, it can result in a tug of war with you the painful loser. If the pot is somewhat soiled and unsightly—break it; it is better to lose a $2 container than a 10-year-old specimen. If a plant simply won't come out of a still-attractive container, try to float it out by using a garden hose to force water through the drainage hole.

A little water

Ages ago, someone concluded that cacti and succulents lived without water; that myth has been incorrectly yet convincingly passed on ever since.

Like all living things, succulent plants need water, though the frequency and amount may be noticeably less than for other plants. Experimenting may be the only way to tell how much water your particular plants need. Here's a good rule: water infrequently, but when you water, do so generously. Use tepid, not cold water. Plants need more water during their growing season than during dormant periods, and it is wrong to try to force them into growth by adding water when they are resting.

A fast-draining soil that dries out slightly between waterings is essential to prevent rotting. Large pots hold moisture for several days whereas small pots may dry out in a day. Remember that clay pots dry out faster than plastic or glazed ones, and that plants in dry, sunny locations or windy areas need more water than those in cool, protected places.

What about fertilizing?

Much has been written about whether or not to fertilize cacti and succulents. Many authorities advocate regular feedings, while others feel this is unnecessary. Most succulent plants can grow satisfactorily without additional nutrients, provided their soil is rich enough. Occasional feedings in the form of bonemeal (1 teaspoon per 6-inch pot) or a liquid fertilizer (a weak solution of a 10-10-10 fertilizer and water) can be given.

Remember that you should fertilize only when plants are actively growing—usually in spring or summer—and not at all during the rest period. Many species take a complete rest in winter, and additional fertilizer at that time would harm them.

Some tree-dwelling kinds of epiphyllum and zygo-cactus benefit from more regular feedings, especially during their prolific blooming season (May through August). Because they may absorb nutrients through their stems and leaves, an overhead spraying of water soluble fertilizer is also helpful.

Plants need to rest, too

Just like people, succulent plants require rest. At one time of the year (usually winter), they enter a period of dormancy. This lull in activity is essential to their health and a natural part of their life cycle.

During this rest period, move plants to a cool place, about 40°F., and water sparingly. The soil should be dry between applications; some cacti require no more than a bimonthly light watering. Do not feed or disturb them—you could cause abnormal growth, expose them to rot, or damage them so that they fail to bloom the following year.

Lasting from 1 month to several months, the rest period differs among individual plants. They will give you hints when regular watering and warmer temperatures are once again needed; fresh growth is evident and the entire appearance of the plant perks up.

Exceptions to the need for a winter rest period are the shade-loving and tree-dwelling cacti like epiphyllums and the Christmas cacti species, along with the fleshy-leafed succulents not native to desert areas. These plants enjoy regular watering throughout the year. The plant's native habitat should be your guide to necessary seasonal changes in moisture requirements.

So your plant has a problem?

Cacti and succulents are remarkably free from most plant ills. Their very nature—strong succulent stems and spiny exteriors—makes them tough and uninviting. Though insects can attack these plants, it is rare.

Since good cultural practices are necessary for healthy plants, a well-cared-for plant is seldom attacked by pests and disease. If a plant is not doing well, don't immediately conclude that it is plagued with insects or a victim of a disease. Most likely, something is wrong with the plant's growing conditions. Check your culture methods before you buy remedies.

Look for signs that indicate a plant is not getting the conditions it needs to prosper. Many times, plants will perk up considerably if you simply move them to another location; they may have been in a draft or in an area without sufficient light for a healthy existence. A gradual yellowing of the foliage, green stems that turn brown, abnormal elongated growth, or soft, mushy stems—these are all obvious signs of problems that might be corrected.

The chart on the next page lists the most common problems associated with less-than-adequate care of succulents and cacti. Unless you actually can see insects on your plants, you'll probably find the cause of poor growth listed on the chart. First, look in the left-hand column for possible abnormalities; then read across to find the cause and, finally, the remedy.

Controlling insect pests

Though damage caused by common insect pests is easily recognizable, the insects are usually small and

Common Plant Problems

Symptom	Probable Cause	Remedy
Failure to make new growth	Too much water, or soil is compacted; roots may be decayed	Repot in fresh soil mix; adjust water practices
Stems or leaves are yellow	Plant is too dry and gets too much heat	Provide better ventilation and more humidity
Stems or leaves *turn* yellow	Possible iron deficiency from soil being too alkaline	Test pH of soil; you may need to add iron
Pale color on new growth	Root injury	Trim away dead or damaged roots; repot plant
Elongated growth	Not enough light	Move plant to location with more light
Failure to bloom, or very few flowers produced	Plant has received too much nitrogen, or winter rest period hasn't been given	Use fertilizer lower in nitrogen, higher in phosphorus; give plants winter rest
Flower buds drop	Temperature is too low or fluctuates too much; plant may be in draft	Move plant to warmer, draft-free location
Soft or mushy growth	Too much moisture; temperature too low	Reduce moisture; cut away soft or mushy parts and dust cuts with fungicide
Corky skin on stems	A natural development on some cacti as they age	
Plant has glassy, translucent look beginning in fall or winter	Frost damage	No cure for damage done; stems and leaves should be removed. Keep plant dry and be sure it is not subjected to low temperatures

hard to see because they hide in leaf joints, flower buds, or soil. It is necessary to inspect at regular intervals, any plant not growing properly. If you find pests, isolate the plant immediately so surrounding plants will not be infected.

Know what you're fighting. Try to determine just what kind of insect has invaded a plant before going out to buy a remedy. There are some general insecticides that take care of many kinds of insects. Soap and water will eradicate some. Nicotine sulfate, one of the best remedies, is safe for indoor use and eliminates a common plant problem—aphids.

This is a list of common insects:

Aphids: Soft-bodied, green black insects dine on tender leaves, flower buds; plants appear distorted. *Remedy:* Spray with solution of nicotine sulfate. (Water plants a day before applying preparation.)

Mealy bugs: Fuzzy, cottony white insects found on spines, stems, roots. *Remedy:* Spray with solution of malathion for outdoor plants; indoors, spray with solution of half rubbing alcohol and half water. For signs of damage at root level, try a change of soil.

Scale: Brown spots (pinhead size) with hard shell coverings. *Remedy:* Remove with toothpick. For heavy attacks, use malathion or nicotine sulfate.

Snails and slugs: Not really insects but a definite problem. *Remedy:* Scatter metaldehyde bait over soil; then water.

Thrips and red spiders: Telltale yellow or white spots on leaves. *Remedy:* Spray with solution of nicotine sulfate; if necessary, use a mitacide.

Fungus diseases: Overwatering, bruises, and improperly healed cuts are some ways decay can start. *Remedy:* Cut away infected area and destroy; dust wounds with sulfur or special fungicide.

Plants that receive good care are rarely attacked by insects; the poorly tended, weak plant is usually the victim. Try to give all your plants a fighting chance by taking the best possible care of them. Don't apply chemical insect controls, unless you know that your plants *do* have an insect problem. Never follow the theory that if a little insecticide is good, a lot will be better. Always follow directions carefully—and most important, guard children and pets against exposure to insecticides.

Index

Photographers

Glenn Christiansen: 42 top left and bottom left, 47 top left and bottom, 56 top right. **Paul R. Johnson:** 10 top left and bottom left, 15 bottom right, 18 center, 23 top right, 31 top left, 48 top left, 50 top right. **Steve W. Marley:** 10 top center and bottom right, 15 bottom center, 18 top left, top right, bottom left, bottom center, bottom right, 23 top left, bottom left, bottom right, 26 top right, 31 top right and bottom right, 34 bottom left and right, 39 bottom right, 41 top right, 42 top right, 48 bottom left, 50 top left and bottom right, 55 all, 56 bottom, 58 all, 63 all, 64 top, 65 all, 66 bottom left and right, 71 all, 72. **Ells Marugg:** 10 top right, 15 top left, top right, bottom left, 26 top left and bottom, 31 bottom left, 39 top left, center, and right, bottom left, 41 top left, bottom left, bottom right, 42 bottom right, 47 top right, 48 top right and bottom right, 50 bottom left, 56 top left, 57 bottom center and top, 66 top left and right. **Peggy Kuhn Thompson:** 34 top, 64 bottom.